Good With Money

A guide to prioritizing spending, maximizing savings, and traveling more

By Anna Mazurek

Copyright © 2018 Anna Mazurek
All rights reserved
ISBN: 9781724190550

Edited by Miles Walls

Cover Design by Clare Vacha

Dedication

This book is dedicated to all the people who have picked me up at airports, let me crash on their couches, and supported this small-town girl's dream to become a world traveler. I sincerely thank you all!

Table of Contents

Introduction 7
    How to use this book 10
    What inspired my financial philosophy? 12

SECTION 1: Top Money Hacks 15
    10 Steps to Mastering Money 17
    How to Make More Money 36
    The "Frugal" vs. "Cheap" Debate 40
    Fear Setting 43
    17 Ways I Save Money Everyday 46

SECTION 2: Top Savings Hacks 59
    How to Save On Medical Bills & Insurance 60
    How to Pay for College Without Debt 69
    Where to Sell the Stuff You Don't Need 78
    Coupon 101 86

SECTION 3: My Travel Hacks 93
    The Real Cost of Travel 95
    Travel Banking 101 102
        How to Avoid Bank Fees 103
        What Type of Credit Card is Best for Travel? 105
        Rewards Credit Cards 105
        Eight Essential Travel Banking Tips 107

How to Cut Costs on Top Travel Expenses............................ 110

How to Make Money While Traveling................................... 129

Where to Teach English 140

The Art of Slow Travel 143

Conclusion 146

About the Author 148

Acknowledgements 149

Disclaimer 150

Introduction

My alarm went off at 10:30 p.m.

It was pitch black outside, and the temperature was well below freezing.

I dreaded getting out of my sleeping bag. All I wanted to do was fast forward 24 hours until I was back in flip-flops and 80-degree weather. Instead, I forced myself to get dressed in five layers of pants and five jackets before putting on my hiking boots.

It was time to summit Kilimanjaro.

Eight hours later, I posed for a photo with the iconic sign to prove I had climbed the tallest mountain in Africa.

Back in the comfort of my flip-flops, the photo instantly appeared on Instagram.

My life probably looks postcard perfect on Instagram—summiting Kilimanjaro, selfies with llamas in Argentina, and sunrise hikes through Japanese temples.

The trouble with social media is that you never hear the backstory or the moments that lead up to that moment. There's no preface post about what it took to be in that exact spot at that precise moment. There's no citation of the sacrifices I made to get to that point.

This book is that preface: the backstory of my financial philosophy.

I'm 37 years old. I have been 51 countries and lived in five. The first time I stepped on a plane, I was 19. Travel has been my top goal for as long as I can remember. Every single decision and choice I've made in my life has gotten me to this point. Nothing to me was more important than traveling. Life's too short to NOT do the things that make you feel alive, and nothing make me feel more alive than traveling.

News alert: I don't have a trust fund. I'm not rich. I don't sell drugs. I haven't won the lottery.

My average gross income (before taxes and deductions) for the last six years is $30,492.

From 2012 to 2015, I averaged only $20,000 a year. Yet, I bought a car for $9,000 (that I paid for with my savings and a six-month payment plan) and spent two to six months a year traveling even though I was only making $20,000 annually.

I also have a Master's degree and no debt. Not even student loans. Nothing.

How did I afford to travel so much?

The secret is simple: I'm good with money.

How is that possible?

My financial philosophy is relentless and extreme, but it's afforded me a plethora of experiences that are priceless.

I am a freelance photographer and writer. I also teach part-time at a university. I run photo trips for high school students in the summers. I've photographed everything from the Dalai Lama to puffins in Iceland to the Foo Fighters. My work has been published in *Rolling Stone, AFAR, Wall Street Journal,* and *Travel + Leisure*. While this might seem like a cool life, it's a difficult life that involved a lot of sacrifices and unconventional decisions.

Since I don't have a trust fund, I found jobs that paid me to travel. I freelanced for travel/lifestyle magazines, taught English in Thailand, and ran photo trips in Asia, most of which paid for my travel and living expenses. Sometimes I worked three jobs to save money to travel on my own – I was a freelance photographer but I also waited tables and bartended, folded clothes at the mall and taught university photo classes. I cut all unnecessary expenses. No Ubers. No sodas. No new clothes. No excessive eating out.

Every decision I made was for my next adventure. I even rented my friend's living room for $230 a month when I first moved to Austin and slept on an air mattress to save money. (Vagabonds like me don't sign leases.) I have quit countless jobs—even jobs that I loved—to travel.

Do you have to work three jobs to be able to afford to travel or achieve your savings goals? Do you have to quit your job and sleep on an air mattress in your friend's living room in order to save money? Do you have to do exactly what I did? Absolutely not.

How to use this book

Since I believe in full transparency and honesty, my goal for writing this book to provide a guide to explain how I funded all of my travels and my life with no debt. These tactics apply to any life savings goal like buying a house or saving for college, not just travel.

As I said, I'm a travel photographer and writer. I don't accept "free" press trips because it's unrealistic for me to be writing about things I can't even afford to do myself. It just feels fake.

In this book, I outline my financial philosophy and discuss the people and experiences that honed my skills. Keep in mind that I am pretty extreme—I saved 50% of my income for the last two years—but no matter your situation or goals, the tactics in this book are universal. Some are based on tried-and-true common sense and others I discovered through research and experience.

My goal is for you to take away skills that apply to your circumstances to help you reevaluate your finances and redefine your priorities to allow you to achieve your financial goals, whether that's traveling for a year, buying a new house or starting that llama petting zoo business you have been dreaming about for years.

This book is NOT a guide to investing. Instead, this book is to help you understand your current financial situation, find ways to maximize your savings with the money you already have and learn how to go make more money.

Taking control of your finances does not mean you're doomed to eat peanut butter sandwiches or instant noodles for eternity. It means making informed decisions and being aware of your income and spending.

Taking control of your finances is the ultimate form of freedom. For me, it allows me to travel long-term. You can use this freedom to chase after the things you care about—starting your own business, paying for your children to go to college or taking that trip to Italy that you've always dreamed about.

Nothing worthwhile is ever easy. Yes, I've invested a lot of time into the art of saving and maximizing my income. Lucky for you, I've done the dirty work for you. Consider this book a treasure map with a clearly dotted line leading you to the giant red X mark over your savings goals. Like a treasure hunt, there will be surprises and possible delays, but you'll still get to the end with determination and relentless persistence.

What inspired my financial philosophy?

My financial philosophy is derived partly from the Buddhist ideal of focusing on a larger goal instead of short-term comfort. In the finance world, it's often referred to as conscious spending, which is the idea that you indulge in the things you love and relentlessly cut your spending elsewhere.

Travel was always the larger goal for me. It came before everything.

I grew up on a farm in South Carolina. My parents own a furniture store and my dad makes 18th century furniture for a living. My dad is a Polish Catholic but was born in East Germany in 1946. My grandparents, my father and my aunt all escaped from East Germany with literally just the clothes on their backs and immigrated to the U.S. when he was eight years old. [I'll save that story for another book.] My dad grew up very poor but made the most of what they had.

As a result, my dad is still very minimalistic, can't stand being wasteful and avoids debt. He saves the scraps from all of his furniture projects to make small side tables and nightstands. By doing this, he cuts down the cost of his materials and wastes very little. He is the happiest person I know, which I believe is directly associated with his priorities that were a result of growing up poor. My observations about my dad and his philosophy on life have shaped my decisions. He only buys the things he needs and nothing frivolous. His spending habits are directly aligned with his goals. He has two pairs of shoes — one for work and one for church. He does invest money in quality tools for his shop, but people love his positivity so much they often give him spare tools they don't need. "If it costs money, we don't need it" is one of his famous lines.

Scholarships funded both my undergraduate and graduate degrees. After I graduated, I knew I would have to fund everything myself since my parents were helping raise my nephew and put my sister through college.

The recession in 2008 was both a wonderful and painful teacher. Prior to the recession, I was freelancing full-time, getting paid to travel and making more money than I'd ever made. When the economy tanked, the majority of my income disappeared, which was a harsh lesson. I moved to Australia on a work visa and spent the year traveling. It was a bold move in uncertain times, but it was one of the first steps to my traveling life. I went from having Hilton Diamond status to living in hostels. In order to survive the recession and focus on my career/travel goals, I had to adjust my finance and spending habits.

I've always had a random assortment of jobs. In Australia, I worked at a bar with a great view of Sydney Harbor and the opera house. At the same time, I freelanced for *Rolling Stone* magazine shooting music festivals and writing about local musicians. *Rolling Stone* would mail my paychecks to my house addressed to "Anna Mazurek Photography (ATTN: Accounts Receivable)", which was hilarious since I was both the photographer, janitor and accounts receivable all in one.

Retail jobs also helped me through tough times and funded my travels. I've folded my share of T-shirts and jeans. These jobs taught me a lot of self control. Even with a 40 percent discount, I couldn't afford to buy clothes all the time. After years of working in retail and denying myself the instant gratification of buying each new thing, I built a mindset where I never really bought anything or nor did I crave anything because most of the things I wanted, I didn't need. They were impractical. In some ways, I suppose you could say I reached "retail enlightenment."

My entire life is based on freedom. I hate being told what to do. I've always followed the unconventional route. There's nothing that can hinder freedom more than debt. There's no freedom quite like living below your means.

Each one of these experiences molded my financial philosophy and made me the power saver I am today. I avoid debt at all costs. I prioritize my spending around my goals and needs, instead my wants. I try to cut costs on my expenses with minimal effort.

SECTION 1:
Top Money Hacks

"You're so lucky that you get to travel so much."

"I'm jealous of your life."

"I'm living vicariously through you!"

Let me let you in on a big secret: Travel has nothing to do with luck. Luck is finding a $10 bill on the sidewalk, not hiking the north shore of Easter Island.

Ever since I was a kid, all I wanted to do is travel. I didn't grow up traveling, but I found a way to make it happen. Eight-year-old Anna would be so proud of 37-year-old me.

To write this book, I sat down and wrote an outline of the steps I used to take control of my finances that allowed me the freedom to follow my dream without any debt. It was an interesting exercise to write this out since I am used to doing these things instinctively.

This section covers my top money hacks including:

- 10 Steps to Mastering Money
- How to Make More Money
- The "Frugal" vs. "Cheap" Debate
- Fear Setting
- 17 Ways I Save Money Everyday

10 Steps to Mastering Money

1. Priorities

The great paradox of life is the relationship between money and time. You either have an abundance of one or a shortage of the other. Write down a list of your top two or three priorities. (For me, it's travel and food. All of my money goes to both of these.)

Find ways to make time or funding for them. Eliminate anything that gets in the way. Sometimes this means eliminating things you want to do – saying no to a dinner with a friend in order to work on a personal project or to save money. Follow the 80/20 rule: Invest your time in 20 percent of your actions that provide 80 percent of the results in your life. Invest your money in the 20 percent of things and goals that bring you joy. Your priorities must align with your values.

Pull out a piece of paper and make a list. Seriously, do it right now.

2. Do the Math.

Don't worry—this isn't long division. This just takes two easy steps:

Step 1: Figure out how much money you are making per month. Look at your pay stub or your last tax return. Write this down.

Step 2: Where is your money going?

The first step to understanding your finances is to understand how much money you have coming in and where it's all going. While this might sound as fun as scrubbing your bathtub, it doesn't really have to be that hard.

Start with your banking or credit card statements. Many banks and credit cards include an online feature that will analyze where you are spending your money to give you an idea.

If you're a very analytical person like me, then you can track all your expenses in a budget tracking apps like Dollarbird (free), You Need a Budget and Mint.com. I initially did this to see where my money was going for a few months. Once I got a good understanding of my finances, I stopped tracking every penny. Although, I did track my spending for the entirety of my seven-month trip in Latin America in 2014 and 2015 to prove that travel isn't as expensive as you think. (It was the most expensive trip I've ever been on and it only cost me $1,300/month!)

Wants versus Needs

After you have a clear idea of how much money is coming in and where it's all going, you can start to shift your spending to focus on your priorities. The best way to start this process is to make a two-column list for "needs" and "wants." Include EVERYTHING: rent, utilities, cell phone, student loans, Netflix, etc. in the appropriate column. The "needs" column should only include housing, food, transportation and healthcare. Everything else, even your MLB.com subscription, is frivolous.

Dealing with Debt

Many of the topics in this list can be applied to save money to put towards debt. If you have a high amount of debt, I recommend checking out financial guru Dave Ramsey's book "The Total Money Makeover" from the library or listening to his podcasts.

3. Trim the Excess

Ask yourself: Where can I cut unnecessary expenses? This is where you need a little tough love and possibly a magnifying glass. You know that gym membership you pay for but haven't used in the last year? Cancel it or start going to the gym. Don't pay for anything you don't use. If you sign up for a free trial of something, set a reminder on your phone to cancel the free trial so you don't pay for things you don't want or need.

Where can you cut expenses? Remember "needs" versus

"wants." You NEED a place to live, but you won't die if you cancel your Amazon Prime membership. Can you share a Netflix/MLB/Pandora account with your family or roommate? Find a cheaper gym/apartment/car insurance plan. Get a roommate. Rent out your spare room. Move into your friend's spare room. House/pet sit. The options are endless. Get creative. How bad do you want to start your own business, travel or buy a house? How bad do you want to get out of debt? Yes, it might be rough for a bit, but if you stick your goals, it will only be temporary.

Start with the basics: Food, shelter and transportation are needs. You probably need a phone, but you don't NEED a $1,000 iPhone XS. (I still have an iPhone 6S.) Does that make sense?

Maybe this means you only go out to lunch on Fridays instead of three days a week. Avoid foolish debt. Foolish debt is debt caused by things you don't actually need: excessively buying clothes, electronics or a car that costs more than you can afford.

Working in retail for most of my life gave me a thick skin. I got to a point when I rarely bought anything at the places I worked because my self control was on point. If it was something I truly needed, then I would spend the money.

There are also apps like TRIM (*asktrim.com*) and Clarity Money (*claritymoney.com*) that will analyze your credit card statements for reoccurring payments and help you cancel things you don't want/need without much effort from you.

4. Prioritize Your Spending

Let's have a little heart-to-heart about what percentage of your income should be going where.

Follow the 50/30/20[1] rule. Think of this as a loose guideline.

- 50 percent of your gross income should go to needs (groceries, rent, gas). Of this 50 percent, no more than 25 percent should go toward rent. (This assumes that you are paying a car payment.) The U.S. government considers households paying more than 30 percent of income on housing to be rent burdened, making it hard for them to afford food and other necessities.

- 30 percent of your income on wants (i.e. things you can live without: fancy vacations; shopping sprees, going to a movie)

- 20 percent of your income should go to savings and debt reduction. This also includes your emergency fund, which should be roughly three to six months of normal expenses. The goal of this fund is to cover any unexpected emergencies like car repairs or just general living expenses if you were to lose your job.

How I Prioritize My Spending

- I practice conscious spending and utilize my money for the things I love. I love travel, food, things that have llamas on

---

[1] https://www.chase.com/news/121817-budgeting-your-money

them and craft beer. That's where my money goes AFTER I pay my bills.

- Since I prefer long-term travel, I don't buy anything six months before a big trip that isn't for that trip because it's my priority. Focus on the things you identified as your top priorities and only spend money on those things. If you are buying a house, don't spend money on anything frivolous that's not going toward the house or saving for the house.

- One of the beautiful things about being in my 30s is that my friends are buying houses, which means they have a spare room that I like to call the "Anna Room." For the last 10 years, I've rented the spare room at many of my friends' houses. It helps them pay their mortgage and helps me avoid signing a lease. (I haven't signed a lease since 2008.) Aside from my brief six-month stint in California, the highest rent I've paid in the last ten years was $505/month including utilities.

- I normally save about 50 percent of my income because I am extreme.

- I hate sushi. Trust me, I've tried to like it, but I just don't. When my friends go to eat at a fancy sushi place, I don't go. Only spend money on things you enjoy. It's silly to waste money on nonessential things that don't make you happy. If my friends are going to a place out of my price point, I either get an appetizer or meet them for a beer afterward.

- Like many young folks, I dreamed of living in Southern California. I quickly found that the reality was nothing like my daydreams. Taxes, gas and rent prices were insane. Everyone I met while living there treated debt as if it was a necessary part of life. I fled to Texas, which has no state income tax, cheaper rent and gas prices. It was one of the best decisions of my life. (I would have moved to Portland but it was too cold.) This is the same reason many people move to the suburbs when they start a family. If you can't afford where you live following the 50/30/20 rule, move somewhere cheaper.

5. Automate Your Bills

I allot a certain amount of my income to savings. When I get paid, I transfer that money immediately. Set up all of your bills to be drafted immediately out of your bank account on payday. If you want the credit card points like I do, then pay your credit card bill in full first thing on payday. Don't forget to allot a certain amount to savings as well. Don't be like my old roommate who never had money to pay the electric bill but always got her car detailed.

If credit cards get you in trouble, then pay for everything in cash. Credit cards lead to greater amounts of impulse buying. Studies by Dun & Bradstreet show that people spend 12 to 18 percent more when paying with a card than cash.

6. Excuse vs. Challenges

"I don't have the time."

"I'm too tired!"

Those are both excuses AND challenges. Review

the priorities you set in Step 1. Your priorities are the things you put first.

Even when I was working three jobs and 14-hour days, I always made the time to plan my meals so I wasn't continually eating out. I would either cook a big meal that would provide several days' worth of leftovers, pack a sandwich for lunch or eat something fast and cheap like scrambled eggs for lunch at home. I treated myself to nice meals on less busy days when I could fully appreciate them. Even though I was exhausted, I still made the time to plan my meals because it was healthier for both my body and budget.

Advertising hotshot Debbie Millman says it best: "Busy is a decision. You don't find the time to do things, you make the time to do things."

7. When to Splurge

Any type of splurge should be directly aligned with your priorities. You can't deny yourself completely of things that make you happy.

Here are four examples of my splurges:

1. When I got back from my year of traveling in 2009, I was broke. By broke, I mean literally living-on-my-credit-card broke, which was a combination of a lot of factors and bad luck (stolen wallet in Thailand). I only lived on a credit card for a few weeks and paid it off in a few months. During that time, I was living very frugally and only allowed myself to eat out once a

week on Sundays for brunch. (There's nothing I love more than BRUNCH!) I let myself spend a whole $20 every Sunday on brunch as a treat, which was a lot considering I literally was living paycheck to paycheck on a $20,000/year salary.

2. For my Kilimanjaro trek, I splurged on quality hiking gear including Patagonia thermals, which got me through that trek and can be reused for winters to come. Everything I bought was on sale and came with an excellent warranty.

3. If paying a small amount of money extra ($10-20) on occasion will make your life easier, then do it. I just paid $10 extra for an overnight bus trip in Chile for a spot on a bus that has full beds instead of regular seats.

4. When I travel, I will splurge in situations where safety is a concern. I will book a private taxi or drop a few extra dollars on a flight that arrives during the day instead of late at night. There's no price for safety.

8. Make More Money

If you need more money, go out and make more money. It's really that simple.

Get a bar job, deliver pizza or start an Etsy business. If you have a financial background and don't mind the risk, start investing in the stock market. The options are endless. Bartending and waiting tables funded the majority of my travels in the beginning. I loved the bar world and met some amazing people.

Financial guru Dave Ramsey mentions a story in one of his books about a man who delivered pizza to get out of debt. It works the same for traveling.

What pays the bills doesn't define you. You should always be working toward a larger goal. Let that overarching goal define you. Who cares if your neighbor judges you for delivering his pizza? When he sees your African safari photos on Facebook, he'll be delivering pizzas with you.

I've included an entire section titled "Make More Money" later in the book that outlines how I did exactly that.

9. Maximize Your Savings

According to Reuters[2], the savings rate in 2017 dropped to 2.4 percent, which is the lowest level in the U.S. in 10 years. Bottom line: People just can't be bothered to save money.

In order to maximize your savings, you need to set clear, attainable goals. Aside from transferring a certain percentage of your income to your savings account, there are many other

---

[2]https://www.reuters.com/article/us-usa-economy-spending/u-s-consumer-spending-rises-savings-fall-to-10-year-low-idUSKBN1FI1NJ

tactics that can help adjust your mindset and habits to allow you to save on everyday expenses.

Coupons & Sales

I am a total couponer. It's very rare that I buy anything that's not on sale. The savings really add up and make a huge difference in my income. I've included an entire section called "Couponing 101" later in the book that outlines my philosophy.

Minimalism

The movie "Fight Club" was right. The things you own, own you.

I believe it's better to invest in experiences, and there are studies[3] that back me up. There's a new car/iPhone released every year, but there's nothing that will replace my travel adventures. I'd rather be the old person with tons of cool stories than a house full of useless junk that my nephew will have to sort through after I'm gone.

The best way to be a minimalist is to imagine that you have to move out of your home every year. What items would you toss? What things would you keep? What things would you resent having and find annoying to move? Keep this mindset

---

[3] https://doi.org/10.1080/17439760.2014.898316

when you are buying new things.

As a full-time traveler, I've learned how much my luggage controls me and my mood. I've come a long way from being the girl in Paddington Station in London with two GIANT rolling bags and two carry-ons who kept tripping over her bags.

After spending a year living out of a suitcase in Australia, I was disgusted by the *stuff* I owned. I started decluttering and selling things. If you are having trouble decluttering or have a bit of the packrat gene like my family, I suggest checking out the book (or eBook) titled "The Life Changing Magic of Tidying Up" by Marie Kondo from your local library. Her basic philosophy is simple: only keep the things that bring you joy.

By fully embracing minimalism, you'll be more conscious of your spending habits.

Don't be Wasteful

I have worked countless retail jobs, and the scene is always the same. There is always a table in the break room filled with tall Starbucks drinks filled almost to the top that were abandoned by employees who didn't have time to drink them before work so they left them for later. At the end of the day, those same cups—still filled to the brim— were left to clutter the table or worse, left in the fridge for days until someone either knocked them over by mistake or threw them out. I sat there every day calculating the wasted money. This cycle repeated every *single* day. If you don't have time to drink your coffee when it's fresh, don't buy it. The moral of the story: don't be wasteful.

Sell Everything

I admit it. I collected Hard Rock Café shot glasses when I first started traveling. It seemed like a cool thing to do. (Thirty-seven-year-old Anna is rolling her eyes at 18-year-old Anna.) They sat on a bookshelf at my parent's house accumulating dust for years, while I was living in other places. One day, I put them in shoeboxes. Six years later, I decided it was time to sell them on eBay. Most sold instantly, and I got back most of my money.

Your old Troll doll collection that's sitting in your mom's basement could be eBay gold. For a list of the best places to sell your excess stuff, check out Section 2 in this book.

Return Things

Don't like that new shampoo you bought at Target? Never worn those jeans from American Eagle? Never opened that "Grey's Anatomy" DVD? RETURN IT!

Most major retailers will allow you to return products that are brand new, defective or sometimes ones you simply don't like for either a refund or store credit. I literally just returned a bunch of brand new books and DVDs still wrapped in plastic that I found at my parent's house from Target. Target gave me a $140 gift card since I didn't have the receipt!

If the return window has passed and you have the receipt, most stores will give you store credit. If you don't have a receipt, some stores limit how much you can return annually. It varies by store and even the location. What if you don't need the gift card? Sell it to a friend or online.

Be courteous: don't use the entire bottle of shampoo and try to return it saying you didn't like it. Don't try to scam people or take advantage of local businesses just to save a few dollars.

If you have a bad habit of buying things and never using them, consider shopping at stores with flexible or lengthy return policies. American Eagle will let you return items at anytime for a refund even a year later! REI has a year return policy. Target's policy is 90 days (120 if you have their REDcard debit or credit card).

Keep Track of Warranties

Before my first long-term trip, I searched forever for the perfect camera backpack. Nothing would fit my camera efficiently. I settled on a hiking day pack with a laptop sleeve made by Osprey that I bought at a hiking store for $100. After three trips around the world, it finally started to rip so I went to buy another one. I asked the staff at the same outdoor store if they had a similar model. Then, the angels started singing and he said, "Call Osprey, and they will fix it for free. They have a lifetime warranty." I sent it to Osprey who, indeed, fixed it at no cost. After sending it back for a few more repairs, they decided it couldn't be fixed and replaced it for FREE. They are literally the nicest folks and have the best customer service. They have my loyalty for life.

The lesson here is to invest in quality gear with warranties. Here is a list of a few other things that I've had replaced under warranty: Marmot replaced my five-year-old $100 raincoat when the lining ripped, Western Digital and LaCie have replaced three external hard drives that crashed, Patagonia just replaced my thermals that were unraveling at the seams and Energizer sent me a refund for my AA battery charger after it started smoking one day. Apple has fixed and/or replaced every Mac and iPhone I've ever had under warranty. (Always buy the AppleCare. Trust me, it's worth it!)

Negotiate

The markets in Asia transformed me into an excellent negotiator. If you've noticed your internet or car insurance bill increasing, then call to negotiate. Be nice and explain the situation. Tell them you've been a customer for XX number of years, money is tight and ask if there's any way for them to lower the bill. This is also a good way to make sure there's nothing extra on your bill that you don't need that can be excluded. It's very important that you understand exactly what you are paying for. You'd be surprised how many companies are willing to negotiate to keep long-term customers! I just got my car insurance lowered by $20 a month by doing this!

Price Shop for Big Ticket Items

The New York Times[4] recently reported that people tend to put too much effort into saving on inexpensive items and not enough on expensive ones. You should spend more time pricing your flat screen TV or car than your toilet paper.

---

[4]https://www.nytimes.com/2016/02/14/upshot/the-rich-can-learn-from-the-poor-in-how-to-be-frugal.html

Buy the Store Brand

Store brands are always cheaper for everything from medicine to spinach. If it's horrible, then return it and get the one you normally buy. The only exception for me is yogurt, pickles and Band-Aids, which are worth the extra dollar or fifty cents for the real ones.

Military Discount

Many places offer military discounts ranging from movie theaters to Apple retail stores. If you are in the military or you are a veteran, then sign up for USAA. USAA provides insurance, banking, investing and real estate services for military members and their families. Most of their services are an excellent deal and cheaper than other suppliers, especially if you bundle their services together. (Since my dad is a veteran, I was able to sign up for USAA.)

Cross Company Discounts

There are many places that give you a discount based on your membership to various organizations. Target will give you a discount on contacts if you have USAA (20 percent), AAA (10 percent), State Farm insurance (15 percent) or Geico (20 percent). Verizon and other cell phone companies will give you discounts based on your employer.

Other key ways to increase your savings:

- **Make your savings hard to access.** Consider opening an online-only account with no debit card. (I use Barclay's high-interest savings account that has no fees or minimum balance requirements.) While the money can still be transferred online in a few days, it takes more effort making it less appealing.

- **Keep Records.** Segment your savings in different accounts or keep a spreadsheet to determine how much money is allotted to specific things (emergency fund, car insurance, etc.).

- **Cut out things you don't use/enjoy.** Don't spend money on any non-essential things that don't enrich your life.

- **Set goals and timelines.** No one wakes up in the morning and decides to run a marathon an hour later. Completing a marathon takes time and training. It's easier to achieve your goals if you have a clear, concise path and goals. Physically write down your goals with deadlines to keep yourself on track.

- **Save any "surprise money."** All birthday gifts, tax refunds, and other unexpected income should go directly into savings.

- **Accountability.** Tell your friends and family about your savings goals. Get a group together and help support each other to achieve your goals. My best friend James uses a free habit and productivity app called Habitica. The app is a game that includes a strong social network along with punishments and rewards that act as motivation.

- **Take advantage of any 401k matching offers.** If your employer matches your contribution, then take advantage. It's essentially free money!

- **Pay in Full:** Many companies allow you to pay monthly for their services, but the rate is almost always cheaper to pay in full. I recently got a 20 percent discount for paying a medical lab bill in full.

- **Fun stuff comes last.** Bills and other essential things like rent must come first. While you should treat yourself on occasion, savings needs to be the top priority. Focus on the higher goal. I live cheap and save like crazy so I can travel long-term and be location independent. (I'm literally typing this from Easter Island.)

- **Find balance.** No one can afford to go out every night. You appreciate eating out more when they aren't daily occurrences. Consider them a treat.

10. Relentless Persistence

I refuse to be ignored. That's how I got hired to shoot for countless magazines. I cold called and emailed until I got a meeting. After the meeting, I stayed on their radar and got access to events I knew they were covering. My persistence got me the job every time.

When something I've been working hard for falls through, I also accept that the timing isn't right. My schedule is simply clearing up so I can focus my time on something else. Regardless, my goal remains the same even though my methods may change. This is the exact same philosophy I apply to my finances. I encourage you to do the same. Nothing worthwhile will ever be easy.

How to Make More Money

"There's no dishonor in having a day job. What is dishonorable is scaring away your creativity by demanding that it pay for your entire existence."
~ Elizabeth Gilbert

After graduate school, I moved to Birmingham, Alabama for an internship at a Time Inc. magazine in 2007. After my first paycheck, it became clear that my $10/hour salary wasn't quite enough. After rent and health insurance, I barely had any money to do any fun stuff. I was 25 years old and tired of eating frozen chicken fingers for dinner every night.

At first, I scrutinized my income and bills to find a way to save money, but I really had no frivolous expenses. Then, I asked Google what to do. Google responded with an article that said, "If you want more money, go make more money." It was so blatantly obvious – I needed a second job!

Instantly, I knew I wanted to work at a bar because people who work at bars are cool. It's one of those coming-of-age experiences that gives you good stories to tell your friends.

And, I knew I couldn't just work at any bar. I had to work at a live music venue and not just any venue—the WorkPlay Theater.

For my Master's project, I produced a photo documentary about a band from Nashville who had recorded an album there and talked about how awesome the venue was. (The venue was started by Alan Hunter, one of the first MTV VJs, and his brothers. Their sound engineer, Davy Moire, toured with Prince and Frank Zappa.) Music photography was my passion, so it made sense to embed myself in the Birmingham music scene.

I walked into the bar after my internship one day and got an application. The next day, I went back with it and talked to the manager, Clay, who is still a really good friend and one of my favorite bosses. He called me a few days later and asked me to work that Saturday night.

I suppose this is where I admit I knew nothing about bartending or waiting tables. My first day on the job was working a private event at the venue with tons of free wine. (I had never opened a bottle of wine in my life before!) I made $250 cash that night, which was more than half of my weekly paycheck from my internship after taxes.

I was so proud of my new "cool" job, but my parents didn't seem thrilled. I believe my dad's response was, "You didn't get a Master's degree to work at a bar." Fast forward to a year later after the 2008 economic crash, I put in my two-week notice to the bar to move to Australia. My parents didn't seem to care that I'd quit my part-time job as a graphic designer at a big newspaper but were appalled I was quitting the bar. "Why are you quitting the bar? You make so much money there!" they asked.

WorkPlay funded the majority of my first long-term trip to Australia. I worked there off and on for five years. Every time I got back from a trip, they put me back on the schedule.

I will dedicate a chapter of my autobiography to WorkPlay, which has been my favorite job of all time and one of the most helpful in my career. (I learned how to shoot music here and met people who helped me build a portfolio that got me hired by *Rolling Stone* magazine in Australia.) The best part about the job was the people. I met so many amazing folks that I'm still friends with to this day.

WorkPlay taught me that life was about the hustle. The people who go after the things they want are the ones who succeed. I truly believe that everyone should work in the service industry at least once. It's a great lesson in humility and makes you an excellent judge of character. (I can't stand people who are rude to waitstaff.)

Above all, WorkPlay taught me that the more sources I have for income, the better. This started the trend of working multiple jobs. It was also a lesson in balance and self-control. Since I had to work another job the next morning, I couldn't go out every night after work. I also couldn't afford to blow my hard-earned money on drinks after work.

My aunt once asked me, "How did you do it?" I had spent years working at the bar and saved a ton of money. My 21-year-old cousin was doing the same but blowing all her money on foolish things. My response was simple: My priorities were in order. I wanted to travel. Nothing else mattered. Nothing was going to stand in my way.

I admit I was embarrassed at times when one of my students or someone I knew professionally came into the bar or mall job I worked at. I struggled with this for years but realized that what pays the bills doesn't define you. The most important thing is that you are working toward a larger goal and have your priorities in order.

Who cares if your friend or neighbor judges you for delivering his pizza or making him a cocktail? When they hear about the car you just paid for with cash, they will be asking if the bar is hiring.

The "Frugal" vs. "Cheap" Debate

The line between frugal and cheap is about as thin as the curtain between first class and coach.

Cheap people buy the type of toilet paper that feels like sandpaper. Frugal people buy the Quilted Northern Ultra Plush on sale with a coupon with their Target Debit Card that saves them an additional 5 percent.

A frugal person buys a large meal at a restaurant and takes home leftovers. A cheap person asks the waitress to box up the food the stranger at the table next to them left on their plate. (Please don't do this — it's totally gross!)

Both cheap and frugal people try to save money but frugal people are focused more on value. Cheap people make decisions on price alone for everything.

Frugality is making a conscious choice to spend money on things you love while cutting your spending on things that you value less.

A few examples:

- Since I am a photographer, I invest in good camera gear and other electronics. While I only buy the gear I need, what I buy is the top of the line — all Nikon branded equipment. I try to get the best price I can or wait for a sale. I also don't buy any gear that I wouldn't use regularly.

- There are two ways to get to the gateway city of Machu Picchu—pay $200 for a roundtrip train, or walk for seven hours down the railway tracks from the last train station. Since I travel with roughly 30 pounds of camera gear, I didn't think twice about buying the train ticket. I did; however, take the bus to the last train stop and book the cheapest train fare. I also paid the $25 for the bus to the entrance gate of Machu Picchu instead getting up at 4 a.m. to hike up the steep stone steps. I knew my gear would weigh me down. I feared I wouldn't make it to the gate in time and miss my chance for a sunrise photo. I was one of the first 20 people inside the gate, and it was worth every penny.

- Every time I buy a new Mac, I upgrade all the specs to the top versions because it's a better value for my money. Too many people buy the standard Mac and outgrow it in six months. For me, spending $200-$500 more means the computer will last twice as long.

Each of these examples was a solid investment focused on my priorities and needs. In hindsight, I have definitely been cheap at times but try my best to lean more toward the frugal side and to make value my top priority.

Dealing with Other People's Priorities

People might not understand your priorities and might call you cheap because it's often extremely difficult to wrap our heads around other people's priorities. Odds are that you have thought someone else was cheap for something they did. The truth is that most of the time we all just have different priorities.

As long as you are paying all your bills, avoiding debt and working toward your goals and priorities, then it doesn't matter what other people think.

Fear Setting

"The hard choices—what we most fear doing, asking, saying—are very often exactly what we need to do."
~ Tim Ferriss

"What we don't often consider is the atrocious cost of the status quo—not changing anything."
~ Tim Ferriss

After graduate school, I was interning at a magazine that promised me I would be traveling and shooting a lot as an intern. While this was true, there were some slow times where I was stuck in the office doing boring work for a few weeks without a photoshoot.

During one of these slow periods, one of the editors had a video shoot on a nearby farm and asked if I wanted to come along to shoot some stock photos. I jumped at the chance to get out of the office. When I got to the farm, he introduced me to the farmer who gave me a golf cart to drive around the farm while I took photos. The farmer's dog, a deaf Jack Russell, jumped up in the passenger's seat to ride with me. That afternoon I spent riding around in that golf cart with a deaf dog was the happiest I'd been in weeks. I knew right then that I wasn't meant for an office job. I needed to travel or at least be outdoors.

A few months later, I decided to take advantage of a new work visa for Americans in Australia. I set a deadline—I would leave when my lease ended in August 2008. Then, something crazy happened—I got hired to work for a newspaper part-time as a graphic designer *and* I got hired as a contract photographer for *Southern Living* magazine. The newspaper job didn't really have set hours. I just had to have my sections done by Monday morning. I was on the road shooting for *Southern Living* two weeks a month and still working the bar job I loved so much. I was making a lot of money, more money than I'd ever made. I saved $10,000 in eight months without even trying.

Then, the recession hit and *Southern Living* stopped giving me shoots. Buyouts started at the newspaper, and morale was low. This made it easier to leave for Australia. I quit everything—the bar I loved, the newspaper, and my freelance photography side work. It was a bold move in uncertain times.

I had a heart-to-heart chat with myself. There would be no more living on expense accounts or in hotels. I'd lose my status as a Diamond member of the Hilton Honors club. I would be living in hostels and working a bar job in Sydney with a huge pay cut. Things were changing.

At this time, I discovered a book called *The 4-Hour*

Workweek by Tim Ferriss, which helped instigate my move. He talked about a tactic called "fear setting," in which you define fears instead of goals and analyze the cost of inaction. You weigh your fears and come up with possible outcomes and ways you would deal with the worst-case scenario. I did exactly that.

I went back to living like I did in college. I ate cheaply. I hardly bought any new clothes for almost a year. Guess what happened? Nothing horrible. I know I can live like that again if I have to. While it wouldn't be fun, I could handle it.

I left all of my jobs on good terms with my employers. The bar agreed to take me back when I returned from my trip. I got hired by the newspaper later to freelance. Having *Southern Living* on my resume lead to other photo work at big publications.

That adventure was a huge risk, but it set the tone for my current career as a travel writer and photographer. I regret nothing.

Here is my question to you: What is the cost of inaction to you if you don't take control of your finances and focus on doing the things you love?

If you need more inspiration, I encourage you to watch Tim Ferriss' TED talk[5] about why you should define your fears instead of your goals.

---

[5] https://www.ted.com/speakers/tim_ferriss

17 Ways I Save Money Everyday

I started writing this book in Buenos Aires, Argentina, in January 2018 and planned to be on the road for an entire year. I have spent the last three years saving and designing my life in a way that I can travel nonstop and work from the road. I take the time to do the research and other things that most people can't be bothered to do so I can have the experiences most people won't have. I'm going to share some of my secrets to help you find ways to save.

1. Avoid Bank Fees

When I first started traveling, I was annoyed by all the ATM fees. My bank would charge me a fee, and the ATM I used would also charge me a fee. Nowadays, ATMs that don't charge fees are a rare and extinct breed like the saber-tooth tiger. (The banks in Argentina currently charge you $10 per transaction!)

An expat friend in Singapore told me about Charles Schwab's free High Yield Investor Checking account, which has unlimited refunds for all ATM fees charged by other banks! The account also doesn't have any minimum balance or direct deposit requirements. AND, it gets better—there's also no foreign transaction fees. (This is a one to three percent fee charged by many banks and credit cards to convert the currency for purchases made overseas.) Last month, they refunded $37 in ATM fees!

I only use credit cards that don't charge foreign transaction fees, which includes all Capital One cards, my American Airlines card and Chase Sapphire Reserve. I also pay off my credit cards monthly so I never pay interest.

For more about avoiding bank fees, check out the Travel Banking 101 section.

2. Never Buy Bottled Water

It's common knowledge that plastic is bad for the environment. If the tap water is safe to drink where you are, buy a stainless-steel water bottle. If you hate the flavor of tap water, buy a Brita filter. If you are traveling and the water isn't safe to drink, spend $20 on the Sawyer MINI filter. This saves me a tremendous amount of money each year and keeps plastic out of landfills.

3. Drink Water at Meals

I gave up caffeine and soda almost 10 years ago based on the recommendation of my dentist who always discovered a plethora of new cavities at every visit. It was hard at first but now, I don't crave sodas at all. I drink tap water, beer and milk (breakfast). Aside from the occasional beer, I never buy a drink when I'm eating out. I worked for two different student travel companies who did not allow students to buy drinks with meals during trips. They only provided water. Bottom line: Drinks are expensive. Consider them a treat. (Plus, free refills are an American thing that you rarely find overseas, which makes buying a drink *even less* economical.)

4. Go to the Library

News flash: Libraries still exist! When I'm not traveling, I'm horrible about reading books in a timely manner so I started checking books out of the library instead. This forced me to read them in less than three weeks and cut down on the clutter in my house. Libraries also offer free online access to eBooks, movies and audiobooks on all your electronic devices through apps like Hoopla and OverDrive. These are all compatible with Kindles, iPads and smartphones. I just met two girls from San Francisco who are reading eBooks from the library on their Kindles while they are traveling in South America! I'm doing exactly the same thing on my iPhone!

5. Buy a Used Car

Forget what the neighbors think. Let's look at the facts: a new car loses 20 percent of its value the minute you drive it off the lot. You can buy a really nice used car for a fraction of the cost. In 2011, I bought a 2009 Kia Spectra with 12,000 miles on it for $9,000 from an ad in the paper. Her name is Betty, and she's an awesome car. Betty travels with me when I'm in the

U.S. and hangs out with my parents when I'm abroad.

6. Conscious Eating Out & Meal Planning

I only like to spend money on things I enjoy, especially when it comes to eating out. Even when I was working 14-hour days spread between three jobs, I made a conscious effort to plan my meals so I wasn't eating out too much, which is both expensive and usually unhealthy. Plus, you never get to enjoy a good meal out when you are rushing between jobs.

I made sure I cooked a big meal once during the week so I had left overs to eat between jobs or I made a quick sandwich or scrambled eggs. On occasion, I'd go to Panera Bread. I also would keep snacks in my car especially on road trips to keep the hanger away.

I worked several mall jobs and couldn't fathom how many employees were spending almost an hour's wage eating out for lunch! Sure, you should treat yourself every so often but not every single day! I made sandwiches every day. (I make amazing sandwiches that both the managers and my co-workers envied! Honey-wheat bread piled high with Boar's Head Honey Maple Turkey, provolone, baby spinach, sliced cherry tomatoes, mayonnaise and avocado. Yum!)

7. Understand Your Insurance

The number one rule for insurance: insure what you can't afford to pay yourself. It's extremely important to fully understand any type of insurance policy you have and confirm your benefits to make sure you aren't paying for things you don't need and so you don't end up with surprise bills. Make sure you read the fine print to understand conditions, deductibles or copays. The goal of every insurance company is to make money; they are not looking out for you.

With health insurance, it's crucial to make sure that you only use in-network services and confirm non-emergency services in advance. For a detailed account of how to save money on health insurance, refer to the detailed guide in Section 2: Top Savings Hacks.

8. Don't Buy Gifts

When you are a travel photographer, people buy you photo albums, journals, passport covers and lots of unpractical items like flip-flop shaped playing cards, which—for the record—are impossible to play any card game with. It made me realize that I was also giving people lots of impractical gifts as well out of obligation. It just felt so wasteful.

I stopped buying Christmas gifts over 10 years ago except for my nephew. However, I shoot a new Christmas card photo every year featuring Alfred, my globe-trotting gnome who accompanies me on all my trips, and send it to my friends around the world. Last year, I sent about 80 cards to friends, family and my editors. It's not cheap, but its more meaningful and cost-effective than buying gifts. Plus, people look forward to them every year!

For birthdays, I try to buy people dinner or drinks as a present because that's more meaningful. (I *always* send homemade birthday cards!)

I don't buy souvenirs as gifts from my travels unless something really reminds me of a person. When you travel for months on end like I do, it's impractical to be carrying around gifts for everyone. (This is coming from the girl who once bought her dad a bag of coffee in Laos and carried it around for three whole months before going home.) To save you money, time and your sanity, cut back on the gifts you buy. When you do buy them, focus on buying practical items or even donating to charity.

9. Research Warranties

I invest in quality brands that stand by their products. When I have a product that has a defect, I immediately look up the warranty. I will email their customer service with pictures simply asking if it was covered by their warranty. I'm never rude or trying to get something for free. I've had the following products replaced due to defects in the last several years: Osprey ($100 hiking day pack), Marmot ($100 raincoat), Patagonia ($60 thermals), Energizer ($30 battery charger), and Western Digital (two $100+ hard drives). I've taken back items to Target as well even after the return policy if they are truly defective to have them replaced.

10. Return Things

Remember that jacket you bought that you haven't worn that still has the tags on it? We all have items like this in our closets. If you've had something for a while and haven't used it, simply return it. Depending on the return policy, you might still get a refund or at least store credit on a gift card. Sephora even lets you return open items you don't like after the return period for in-store credit. If you don't need the store credit, then sell the gift card to a friend.

If you don't have the receipt, many stores like Target and Walmart will let you return items for store credit without a receipt. There's usually a limit per year, and it can vary by store location.

11. Free Trials

I don't watch TV. It's always seemed like a waste of time so I've never really needed Netflix, Hulu or anything like that. I have signed up for free trials for Netflix DVD and Amazon Prime for specific instances when I wanted it to watch a specific movie or needed to have something shipped in a pinch. I'm currently using a six-month free trial for Amazon Prime, which is available to anyone with an education email address ending in .edu. I've set a reminder in my phone to cancel it when the trial ends. (FYI: Amazon Prime is worthless if you are overseas because you can't stream any movies or ship anything.)

12. Teacher/Student Discount

Education discounts have been a huge help with funding my travels. Most major attractions across the world from Machu Picchu to the Tower of London to nearly all museums offer discounted student/teacher rates. (Please note some have an age limit.)

I've even gotten software (Adobe and Microsoft Office) either free or at a discount through universities where I taught at or attended. Many retail stores also give you student/teacher discounts, including J. Crew (15 percent), Forever 21 (10 percent), Goodwill (10 percent), Banana Republic (15 percent) and Michael's craft stores (teachers only 10 percent). This also includes movie tickets, newspaper subscriptions and travel on Greyhound.

13. Avoid Monthly Payments

The world seems to be going to a monthly payment plan, which I hate. I prefer to just pay for things in advance. Aside from my cell phone bill, car insurance and other unavoidable monthly costs, I limit my monthly subscriptions to just Apple Music and a *New York Times* subscription. I don't have Netflix, Amazon Prime or things like that. If your roommate has Netflix, then share it since you live in the same place and probably share a TV. I feel the same about Amazon Prime since I rarely use it.

I never pay for things I don't use and suggest you do the same. Clarity Money (*claritymoney.com*) and Trim (*asktrim.com*) are great apps I mentioned previously that will analyze your account statements to help you to cancel things you don't use.

14. Take Advantage of Work Benefits

Retail discounts: When I was in grad school, I worked at a clothing store at the mall so I could afford to buy clothes. The employee discount was a huge help. Many stores also offer programs that allow employees to give the discount to their friends. Several friends gave me their discounts to buy a good chunk of my hiking gear for Kilimanjaro.

Retirement Accounts: If your employer matches your 401(k) contributions, then it's silly *not* to take full advantage of it. It's *literally* free money. Plus, saving for retirement is important. Even some part-time retail jobs offer 401(k) matching, so be sure to take advantage and ask about your benefits!

Commuter benefits: Many companies also offer commuter benefits through companies like WageWorks. I had a job that paid $100/month for public transit onto a WageWorks debit card that could only be used for public transport. Since public transport wasn't an option where I lived, I saved the money on the card to use when I traveled. I used it on countless trips for all types of transport ranging from Amtrak trains to Uber to the subway in NYC. It cut the cost of my trips in half.

Health Insurance: For a long time, I worked at a part-time job that gave me amazing health insurance. It saved me a lot of money and covered all my travel vaccinations. Even retail stores like Starbucks and the Apple store offer health insurance plans for part-time employees.

15. Frequent Flyer and Rewards Programs

I am the queen of frequent flyer miles. I use my Chase Sapphire Rewards credit card to pay for everything and pay it off each month. When I travel, I make sure to sign up for rewards programs to collect points/miles. This includes work travel since my travel is often paid for by my job, especially when I'm managing photo trips abroad. I have accounts with all the major U.S. airlines. When I fly one of their sister airlines, I make sure to add my frequent flyer number for the affiliated U.S. airline. The same goes for hotel points. Most of my flights on both of my South American trips were on miles.

I also sign up for loyalty and rewards programs at retail stores like Walgreens. The trick to this is to only buy what you need and don't let these programs force you to overbuy.

16. Maintenance

I once took in two pairs of winter boots for what I thought would be easy repairs. The boot repair man scolded me. Since I'd waited too long to bring in my boots, he would have to replace the heel on both shoes instead of just adding a cap. Even so, getting the heels replaced on two pairs of boots was significantly cheaper ($30) than buying two new pairs of boots.

After being set straight by the boot repair man, I realized all of my shoes were wearing down on the back of the right heel from driving, which is called "driver's foot." I started taking off my shoes when I drive now or wear a cheap pair of flip-flops. My shoes now last significantly longer.

The more you take care of your belongings, the longer they last. I hang many of my clothes to dry so they don't fade in the dryer. I get my oil, transmission fluid and drive belts changed in my car at the correct mileage. All of this saves me money in the long run.

17. Set Spending Limits

I always have a limit in my head for how much I'm willing to spend on a particular thing. For clothes, that limit is $20. The only exceptions are shoes, outdoor gear and winter coats. I try to buy everything on sale so that it's as close to my limit as possible. Most of my everyday clothes come from American Eagle, Target, H&M and Forever 21 so this is easy. It's almost impossible to get outdoor gear for $20, so I look for good sales.

For example, I used the REI member 20% coupon to buy a new pair of $80 prAna hiking pants. (I have two pairs. I bought the first pair in 2013 for $50 on sale.)

My limit is the same for eating out or going out with friends. I try to stay under $20. I'll go over occasionally, but that's usually the target number I keep in mind. Of course, this means I don't eat steak a lot or sushi (gross!). I have friends who repeatedly state they spend too much money on going out to dinner. We will be eating at the same restaurant and my tab is $12 and their tab is $40 or $60!

The thing that really helps me keep my spending limits in check is to divide the cost of an item by the number of hours I'd have to spend working to pay for it. If you make $15/hour, is it worth working for four hours to pay for your $60 brunch? Is a $200 pair of shoes worth working eight hours at a $25/hour job? Do you think working 10 hours a month is worth a $500/month car payment for a $50/hour job? The decision is yours.

SECTION 2:
Top Savings Hacks

I am a planner by nature, which is both a blessing and curse. I am the friend who downloads the GPS map so we don't die on remote hikes. I'm the person who always has a headlamp and snacks. I always research the cheapest, safest way from the train, bus station, or airport to my accommodation.

Being a planner means I do *a lot* of research—an annoying amount. The upside is that it helps me understand a lot of things, from health insurance to the types of material used in lightweight sleeping bags.

In this section, I've compiled a list of my research and hacks to help you save money on some major life expenses without spending the time to do the research.

- How to Save on Medical Bills
- Minimalism (Where to Sell Stuff You Don't Need)
- Couponing 101
- How to Pay for College Without Loans

How to Save On Medical Bills & Insurance

The general rule for insurance is that you insure what you can't afford to pay for yourself. I am diligent about understanding my insurance policies— what's covered and what's not. The more you understand about your insurance, the less surprise bills you will get in the mail.

It is an unfortunate reality in life that every item has a price tag in a retail store but no doctor's office has a set list of prices. The U.S. healthcare system is complicated, confusing and doesn't always have the best interests of the patients in mind.

After a lot of time and research, I've figured out how the system works and lowered my healthcare costs. I've outlined a list of steps to help you do the same. Keep in mind that healthcare is always changing. Despite these changes, most of the tips will still be universal since they focus on larger mechanics that do not often change.

[This chapter was checked for accuracy by a utilization review nurse who reviews charts for insurance companies.]

Understand Your Benefits: In-Network versus Out-of-Network

Review your policy to make sure you fully understand your benefits. Confirm with your insurance company that all doctors and labs are in-network. Make sure you fully understand your financial responsibility for all procedures. Yes, calling your insurance company takes time, but it can save you a fortune in the end.

I call my health insurer before visiting a new doctor to confirm they are in-network. This is *crucial* since many health providers offer NO coverage at all for out-of-network services. (You can check this online but it's often not up-to-date. If you do check online, screenshot the page to have proof that the doctor is insured.) Insurance companies do negotiate rates with in-network services for a fraction of the cost of out-of-network, which is great if you go to an in-network provider. This also means out-of-network rates are *never* discounted. For example, I just had a mole removed by a dermatologist that required a biopsy (it was thankfully benign). An out-of-network lab would have cost me $500-600, but the in-network lab only cost me $82. BIG difference.

WARNING: If you have an emergency, your insurance will often cover your Emergency Room visit, but if the doctor is considered out-of-network, you'll be responsible for the bill. Keep this in mind if you travel between states frequently. Many of the Affordable Care Act policies only offer coverage in the state where you live, which is tricky if you travel a lot. Stay up-to-date on policy changes since healthcare is an ever-evolving industry.

Ask for Procedure Codes

If a doctor orders any blood work or X-rays, I ask for the CPT codes for each. (CPT stands for Current Procedural Terminology, which is set by the American Medical Association and identifies the services performed.) I also get the CPT codes for the office visit.

Insurance companies can look up these codes and tell you what codes are covered. If they aren't covered or if you haven't met your deductible, then they can tell you the negotiated in-network rate. Keep in mind some services are only covered if billed with an office visit so be sure to ask about this!

Do not listen to any doctor or nurse who tells you something will or *should* be covered by insurance. They aren't the ones who determine coverage or set rates. They have nothing to do with that part of the equation. More importantly, they aren't the ones paying the bill. *You* are the one who has to sign the piece of paper saying *you* are financially responsible for the bill, not them.

Take Notes

I keep a spreadsheet on my computer where I document every call I make to any customer service line that includes the date, time, notes on what we discussed, the representative's name and a reference number for the call. I do this for any type of customer service call ranging from my cell phone provider to banking. I make decisions based on the information I am given by the representative. I always repeat back the information to make sure I understand it correctly.

If I am given misinformation by the insurance company that costs me money, I will call them and refute the claim based on the misinformation I was given. I have prevailed every single time because I can pinpoint the exact call and they go listen to the tape and see that I was right. This has saved me hundreds of dollars over the last 15 years!

Pay in Full

I got a 20 percent discount when I paid my recent bill for a biopsy on a mole that was removed. The lab said they do this for everyone who pays in full. It was $82 after the discount. Obviously, if it's a *huge* bill, then this might not be an option. Try your best to pay in full to save yourself money in the long run.

Make Sure Labs are In-Network

Even if your doctor is in-network, they might use an out-of-network lab. If you think there is a chance that you might need lab work done, call the doctor's office and ask what lab they use. You should also call your insurance company to confirm the lab is in-network.

Ask for Generic Medications

While most people are aware of this, it's good to just double-check with your doctor to make sure they write the prescription in the correct way. Many insurance plans will only pay for generics. The GoodRx website (*goodrx.com*) and app will show you the cheapest place to buy medications and lets you search by prescription name.

Prescription Refills by Mail

If your insurance provides the option to get a 90-day supply of meds by mail, then do it. Usually, you only pay 2/3 of the cost for this service. For example, if you normally pay $10 a month for a medicine, then you will only pay $20 for a three-month supply, which saves you $10 every three months.

Check Claims for Accuracy

Throughout my life, I have had X-rays done for various reasons at various doctors through various insurance companies. Often, I was forced to pay out of pocket for services the insurance company stated were not covered, but then the they *still* covered it even though they said they would not. Each time, I've noticed MONTHS later and had to ask for a refund from the doctor's office since I'd paid in full. Each time the doctor claimed they would have gotten around to giving me a refund. Most claims show up on average a month after you have the appointment or procedure. Set a reminder on your phone to check in a month.

Go Overseas

Hear me out before you roll your eyes. These are all true examples based on my experiences and from friends. I'm starting with the most serious.

Scenario #1: Cancer

I went to lunch with one of my teaching colleagues today. He and his wife are both retired and just returned from a trip to the Netherlands. I asked if they went to see the tulips. They laughed. They went for one of his wife's cancer treatments.

She has been fighting a rare form of cancer for years. They have traveled across the world multiple times (Netherlands, Singapore, Germany, etc.) for various treatments for several reasons: it's significantly cheaper and more time efficient. (These were all doctor recommended treatments approved by the FDA.) If she hadn't gone abroad for these treatments and waited to get through all the red tape and bureaucracy of her U.S. medical insurance, she said she probably would have been dead six years ago. Going abroad bought her more time with her family.

Scenario #2: Dentists

Shortly after I moved to California after living in Asia, I went to the dentist immediately after my insurance kicked in. The dental hygienist reprimanded me for not getting my teeth cleaned in over a year.

"I quit my job and didn't have dental insurance," I explained. "Plus, I've been living in Asia for six months."

Her response changed my life: "Why didn't you get your teeth cleaned in Thailand? It's cheap, and they have great dentists." Turns out, she'd lived in Bali for a while and knew the scoop on where to go to the dentist in Asia.

It blew my mind. The next year, I paid $30 to get my teeth cleaned in Bangkok in some of the swankiest dentist offices I've ever seen.

My best friend lives in Tokyo and raves about the dental care. Without insurance, it cost $50 for a filling and cleaning. It costs roughly $250 per filling in the U.S. (Her dentist went to medical school in Oregon, by the way!) This is Japan, not a developing country. It's high-quality medical care for a fraction of the cost!

Scenario # 3: Prescriptions

For about two years, I was cursed with recurring eye infections. The doctor always prescribed the same medicine: Vigamox. It had no generic at the time. It cost almost $200 without insurance and $30 with the good insurance I had at the time. I was in Thailand once and saw Vigamox in the pharmacy for $7 with no insurance. No prescription was needed. It had the same expiration date and batch number as the one I'd gotten in the U.S. (This alone tells you how messed up the healthcare system in the U.S. is currently.) I bought several bottles and brought them home.

Scenario # 4: X-Rays in Thailand

I had X-rays done in Thailand on my hip (a running injury) in the nicest hospital I've ever been in my life: Bumrungrad International Hospital. It was $70. It cost $700 for the same X-rays in California six months prior. The doctor spoke perfect English and spent more time with me than any doctor I've ever visited before. He literally read the X-ray results to me immediately afterwards! Plus, the hospital itself looked like a posh spa.

Scenario #5: Travel Medical Insurance

One of the main reasons I'm traveling for most of this year is the fact that travel medical insurance is a fraction of the cost of U.S. medical insurance.

Since I am self-employed, I have to pay more for my insurance than people who are insured through their jobs. My mid-level insurance plan increased $100 to $437 a month in January before I left for this trip. My current travel medical insurance is $50/month with no deductible. (It would have been $30/month but I paid extra to cover adventure activities.) There are two caveats: It doesn't offer any U.S. coverage, and pre-existing medical conditions are normally not covered. There is a stipulation that covers unexpected occurrences of a pre-existing conditions, which they have covered for me in the past, like the X-rays in Thailand I mentioned above.

When I visit the U.S., I buy a short-term major-medical insurance policy that has a high deductible ($2,500-$10,000 usually) and only offers coverage once the deductible has been met. I recently bought a $150/month policy with a $2,500 deductible with 100 percent co-insurance, which covers everything after the deductible has been met for my upcoming six-week trip to the U.S. this summer. Now, this is only for catastrophic coverage. I plan to get a physical and other regular checkups in Thailand later this year since I just had a physical less than a year ago. (In Thailand, a physical at a fancy private hospital is $170 USD including all bloodwork and a chest X-ray. It costs $36 USD to get your teeth cleaned at the dentist.)

How to Pay for College Without Debt

How did I avoid debt from college?

I grew up in South Carolina, which has scholarships funded by the state lottery. These are still available to every in-state student with a B average or above. I was also awarded university scholarships that are automatically given to applicants who meet specific academic requirements. In addition, I applied for all available departmental scholarships. If there was a scholarship, I applied for it. I worked hard to make sure I had the good grades to meet the requirements. I once won a Budweiser scholarship for $500!

The combination of all those scholarships covered the cost of tuition, housing and a meal plan almost in full. My parents had a small college fund that covered the rest for me (less than $1,000 a semester).

Since I was lucky enough to not have to work a part-time job during school since scholarships covered almost everything, I focused 100 percent on school and graduated with a 3.9 GPA.

For graduate school, I applied as an out-of-state student to the University of Missouri to get a master's degree in photojournalism in late 2004. (Missouri is one of the best journalism schools in the country.) Before applying, I called and asked about funding and scholarships. Turns out, almost all graduate schools have graduate assistantships opportunities, which waive tuition (even out-of-state) and pay a small stipend. (Please note that not all states allow tuition waivers.)

The deadline for assistantships was the week after the university sent out acceptance letters. The minute I got accepted, I applied for the assistantships. I got hired to work as a graphic design teaching assistant on the sports section of the student newspaper. I did this for the first year of graduate school. The stipend portion paid my rent ($325/month including all bills) and there was a little bit left over to help with food costs. (My parents did contribute a small amount to help with my living costs and gas to come home for holidays.) I only had to pay $600 in administration fees each semester for school since the tuition was waived.

On top of that, I applied for departmental scholarships, which offered the same level of funding without the work requirement. I received two of these my last year of graduate school. I kept the same job at the newspaper and was paid $12/hour, which at the time was the most money I'd ever made. (They paid graduate students more than undergrad.) I also got a part-time job at the mall working at a clothing store making $6/hour so I could afford to buy clothes with their 40 percent discount. Essentially, I was in school fulltime and working two jobs on the side just to avoid student loan debt.

Most scholarships will only cover you for four years (undergraduate) and two years (graduate school). This is why I *always* graduated on time. Staying another semester was *never* an option.

Things have changed a bit since then. I have started researching college costs for my 16-year-old nephew and believe that I've found a way to get him through school without debt, providing he keeps his grades high. Keep in mind these take time, but a time investment to do the research is much shorter than the time span it takes to pay back student loans.

Tips for Paying for College Without Debt

1. Research University Scholarships

When you apply to many public universities, you are automatically considered for certain university-funded scholarships that are often merit based. Many universities also offer scholarships for non-freshman in certain majors with an emphasis on STEM majors. Call the financial aid office of the university you want to attend or check their website to research the following questions:

- What is the cost of tuition?
- What funding is offered by the university?
- What are the grade requirements?

- Is scholarship eligibility determined by your standing in college (freshman/sophomore, etc.)?

The more you understand the costs and options available, the easier it is to put a plan together to eliminate debt.

2. Departmental Scholarships

The biggest mistake most students is make is not taking the time to apply for scholarships. I once taught at a university that offered departmental scholarships in the journalism school. Almost every student who applied and met the requirements got a scholarship because so few students applied! Most students either weren't aware of the opportunities or didn't take the time to apply. Most departments will offer scholarships, so check their websites or call the office to ask.

3. External Scholarships

I have a friend who got a left-handed bowling scholarship. Seriously. I couldn't make this up if I tried. There are a ton of databases out there with any type of scholarship you can imagine. Many are listed on the financial aid websites for most major universities as non-institutional scholarships. Popular databases that are recommended by guidance counselors include Fastweb (*fastweb.com*), Cappex (*cappex.org*) and Unigo (*unigo.com*). Criteria for scholarships vary widely from ethnic background to community involvement.

Yes, it takes time to write the applications, but always keep copies of previous essays since they can often be tweaked and used for multiple applications. I constantly tweak old job essays and cover letters, especially those that resulted in my hiring.

4. Take Advantage of Lottery-Based Scholarships

Eight states currently have lottery based scholarships: Arkansas, Florida, Georgia, Kentucky, New Mexico, South Carolina, Tennessee and West Virginia. These programs vary but cover a good portion of in-state tuition for students who have good grades (usually a B average) and meet ACT/SAT score requirements.

5. Apply for Need-Based Grants that Don't Need to be Repaid

The U.S. government offers several need-based grants including the Federal Pell Grant, which is the most popular. The maximum award amount changes annually and student must fill out a Federal Application for Financial Student Aid (FAFSA) form to determine eligibility. To qualify, a student's total family income must be less $50,000. A majority Pell Grant money goes to those with income below $20,000. You should apply even if your family makes between $20,000 and $50,000 a year because even a small award will help! For more information, visit the Federal Student Aid website (*studentaid.ed.gov*).

6. Get a Job (Full or Part-time) That Pays for School

Many employers will pay up to $5,000 a year for their employees to go to school or fund their education. This even includes part-time retail jobs like Starbucks and Apple. Business Insider[6] published a list that also includes Verizon, Home Depot, Intel and Boeing. I have many friends who are doing this right now.

7. Take AP Courses

If you are in high school or your kids are in high school, make sure they take as many AP courses as possible. This could save you the cost of an entire semester of college! I went into college in 1999 with two AP credits which made my course load lighter my senior year and made it easier to study abroad. My nephew just started his junior year and already has three AP credits!

8. Apply for Assistantships for Graduate Programs

Research assistantship programs that waive tuition. By working as a teaching or research assistant or teaching your own class, your tuition can be waived. You will most likely also be paid a stipend. I know people who taught Spanish classes

---

[6] http://www.businessinsider.com/companies-that-will-pay-for-your-tuition-2014-6

that waived their tuition in the journalism program at Mizzou.

9. Live with Family or Six of Your Best Friends

College is not the time to live like a king. Learn to live cheap. Rent out your friend's couch or live with a family member for cheap. Sacrifice now for a larger goal. Plus, this usually means you'll have some hilarious stories to tell when you get older.

10. Avoid Private Schools

It's common knowledge that private schools are insanely expensive. Apply to public schools in your state for cheaper tuition rates. It can't hurt to look at private schools and apply for scholarship opportunities that offer a full-ride just in case.

11. Be Realistic

It's silly to go into over $100,000 worth of debt for a job that only pays $30,000/year. I am not telling you to give up on your dreams, but to be creative and find ways to fund your degree program using the tactics in this list. You can do anything you want in life if you're willing to work hard enough!

12. Loan Forgiveness Programs

If you *must* take out a loan and work in a field like teaching, then you can work at a low-income school to have a portion or all of your student loans waived through two programs: the Teacher Loan Forgiveness Program and Perkins Loan Cancellation for Teachers. For other careers, consider the Public Service Loan Forgiveness Program, which forgives the remaining balance of loans after 10 years of payments while working full-time for a qualifying employer. Visit the U.S. Department of Education's website (studentaid.ed.gov) for more details.

13. Join the Peace Corps to Forgive Student Loans

The Peace Corps is an international volunteer program run by the U.S. government. The program lasts 27 months and places volunteers in various locations across the world to work in six different sectors ranging from agriculture to education to community economic development. There's no age limit. You are paid a stipend and are usually fluent in the local language by the end. Most importantly, federal student loans can be eligible for partial or total cancelation. From the Peace Corps website: "If you have federal student loans, such as Stafford, Perkins, direct, and consolidated loans, you may be eligible for deferment, partial cancellation, income-driven repayment, or eligibility for the Public Loan Service Forgiveness Program during Peace Corps service. Volunteers with Perkins loans may be eligible for a 15–70 percent cancellation benefit." For more details, check out PeaceCorps.gov.

14. Include Student Loans in Salary Negotiation

I had a friend who was hired for a headmaster position at an international school. Part of his job offer was to pay off his graduate school loans ($40,000) in exchange for a lower salary the first few years. Afterwards, his salary jumped tremendously. This is becoming more common in higher-tier jobs and easier to negotiate for graduate and doctoral degrees!

Where to Sell the Stuff You Don't Need

I spent some time over Christmas decluttering my old room at my parents' house and helping them eliminate their own clutter. Where are the best places to sell things? I've compiled a list of places in the U.S. that are best for selling the excess clutter in your house. To maximize efficiency, I'll often drop boxes off at many of these locations, go run errands, and come back to collect my money and any leftover items.

Collectables, Antiques and Just About Anything

- **eBay:** eBay is great for just about anything. I've sold everything from old Mac computers to camera lenses to Harry Potter books on the platform. The company does a great job of making it as easy as possible to list items using their app and uploading photos straight from your phone. No fees are charged until the item sells. They even calculate the shipping for you and give you a discount for purchasing the shipping through them. Pro tips: Photograph your items on a solid white or grey background from literally every angle. Be as clear and concise as possible when describing the condition and details about the item. By doing both of these things, you'll minimize the risk of having any issues.

- **Garage sales:** Put up signs in your neighborhood and lay everything out in your driveway. Post it all over social media including neighborhood Facebook pages and groups. Ask the neighbors if they want to join in!

- **Flea markets:** There's at least one in every town. It's an effective selling platform since people come directly to these spaces looking to spend money. Plenty of people make a living selling at flea markets. This is great if you don't have the space to have a garage sale or yard sale. Focus on renting a booth during the busiest shopping weekends which normally coincide with holidays.

- **Facebook and Facebook Groups:** Chances are you've seen these posts from friends. If you are selling something, post it on Facebook and see if anyone is interested. I sold my old computer last year to a friend's mom for $1,000 after posting it on my personal Facebook profile, which is more than I would have made on eBay with all the fees. (Try to sell electronics on Facebook before listing on eBay, which is still best for collectables and other items than can be easily shipped.) There are also local community Facebook Groups that act as a marketplace for selling specialty items. This is particularly true when it comes to children's toys, clothing, strollers and car seats.

- **Craigslist:** You can find and sell just about anything you want on Craigslist. When I lived in Santa Barbara, this is how I found a place to live. Use common sense with listings and take usual safety precautions. Meet people in public places and for extra safety, meet in the parking lot of a police station.

Where to Sell Clothing

Consignment Shops

- **Locally-run consignment shops:** These are the best options for getting the best amount of money and vary by town, so I can't give exact recommendations. Some buy things directly from you and others sell on consignment, which means you get paid when your items sell. There's one shop called Roundabouts Consignments in Columbia, South Carolina, that I've sold stuff at for years with success. To be exact, I've made $773 in just the last few years at that specific store!

- **Once Upon a Child:** This is the next best option for children's clothing and accessories. They also take sports gear and books. I've sold a lot of my nephew's clothes here for my sister. It's not a huge payout but better than nothing.

- **Plato's Closet:** This store focuses mostly on teen clothing. I've never had much luck at this chain even when I was in college. Maybe my clothes were just not cool enough. If you have teenagers, this should be your first stop. They specialize in girls' sizes 0-30 and men's waist sizes 28-40.

- **Buffalo Exchange:** This chain has 48 stores in 17 states. They pay 30 percent of the selling price for the clothes they buy. You can also opt for a 50 percent payment in store credit. They specialize in both men's and women's clothing and accessories.

Sell Online

- **ThredUp:** This is a popular online retailer that will send you a free bag with free prepaid postage to mail in your clothes, shoes and accessories. This takes minimal effort but pays the lowest rewards—roughly 5-10 percent of the selling price. Commission rates are higher for higher priced items. My friends have had great success with this, but I recently sent in a huge bag and only made $9.41. They do offer an option to send you a free bag that gets donated directly to charity, which is a great option to save you the time of donating it yourself. You just leave the bag outside your home for the USPS to pick up. *(thredup.com)*

- **Poshmark:** This requires a bit more effort than ThredUp but pays higher commissions. (You get 80 percent for all items you sell over $15.) The only catch is that *you* take photos of the items and upload them to the site similar to making an eBay listing. Flat-rate shipping is handled by Poshmark. *(poshmark.com)*.

Books, DVDS, CDS and Video Games

- **Local music stores:** You'll get the most money from local stores. For example, a local music store in Columbia, South Carolina, paid me $3 per CD during my holiday cleanout. A chain store that buys CDs only paid me $1-$1.50 per CD. They often take both CDs and DVDs.

- **Local bookstores:** Local, non-chain bookstores are always best.

- **Local chains:** There's a local chain in Austin, Texas, called Half Price Books. I've sold a few things there, but it wasn't worth my effort. I didn't make enough to justify driving to the store. Call local chains in your area first to discuss their policy to see if it's worth the effort. If there's an overstock of an item, then they are less likely to buy, which is the biggest issue I had.

- **2nd & Charles:** For books, this chain is a good option. If you don't have luck selling your DVDs, CDs and video games elsewhere, then this is your next best option. I literally took in three boxes of old books from my parents' house, along with DVDs they didn't want. They paid me $35 cash for the two boxes they bought. (They would have given me over $50 in store credit, but I didn't need store credit.)

- **eBay & Amazon:** Selling online is another option. The post office lets you ship books at cheaper rates via Media Mail. You can buy cheap mailing envelopes at the Dollar Store to help cut shipping costs. Amazon lets you trade-in old textbooks for Amazon gift cards.

Electronics

Best Buy Trade-In Program: You can sell or recycle your old electronics in exchange for a Best Buy gift card. This includes all brands of smartphones, computers, smart watches, gaming hardware and video games. The current value for my 128GB iPhone 6S is $135.

Target: You can exchange your old electronics for a Target gift card in any Target store with a mobile phone department. They also accept gaming consoles and tablets. They do offer a link to a third-party party to do it online. Values vary by product.

Gazelle: This company will buy smartphones, tablets, Apple computers, and Apple TVs via PayPal, Amazon gift card, or an old-fashioned check. They are offering me the highest amount for my current phone ($155) of all the companies in this list. My friends have all has success with this.

Amazon: You can trade in your items for an Amazon gift card. They accept phones, Kindles, tablets, video games, Bluetooth speakers, and cell phones. Unlocked phones bring the highest rates. My phone is worth $125, which is lower than the other options listed.

Apple: Apple will let you trade in your old Apple products for a gift card. They will also let you recycle any brand of electronics for free through their website. They are offering me a $135 gift card for my phone currently. [7]

---

[7] Apple Trade In Program: https://www.apple.com/shop/trade-in

Old Gift Cards

Target: Any Target store with a mobile phone department will allow you to trade in unused gift cards from other retailers for a Target gift card. Best Buy, Starbucks, Sephora and other larger retailers are the most widely accepted. For a $20 gift card, you can get roughly $11.60 back on a Target gift card.

Gift Card Exchanges: To safely sell old gift cards, check out legitimate gift card exchanges like Giftcards.com, Cardpool, CardKangaroo, CardCash, ABC Gift Cards or Raise.com.[8] Consider searching the online aggregator GiftCardGranny.com to compare deals. Grocery and gas gift cards yielded the highest returns in 2017, according to a 2017 report by GiftCardGranny.com.[9] Some grocery stores have kiosks that will buy them back in store.

Recycle Old Clothes for Discounts

H&M: Bring in a bag of old clothes for recycling and get 15 percent off your next purchase.[10]

Levis: For a bag of clean, dry clothing and shoes, you get a

---

[8] Safely Sell Unwanted Gift Cards:
https://www.nbcnews.com/better/business/how-safely-sell-those-unwanted-gift-cards-ncna838736
[9] GiftCardGranny.com Selling Statistics for 2017:
https://www.giftcardgranny.com/blog/most-resold-gift-cards-2017
[10] H&M Recycling:
https://about.hm.com/en/sustainability/get-involved/recycle-your-clothes.html

20 percent coupon for a single regular-priced item. You can also print a free shipping label to ship your clothes directly to Goodwill for donation.[11]

Madewell: Donate a pair of jeans (any brand) and get $20 off a new pair. [12]

The North Face: Bring in any brand of clothing or footwear to their retail or outlet stores for a $10 coupon off your next $100 purchase. [13]

Patagonia: Trade in Patagonia clothing for credit towards new or used clothing at their retail stores.[14]

---

[11] Levi's Recycle program:
http://www.levistrauss.com/sustainability/planet/#recycling-reuse
[12] Madewell Jean's Program:
https://www.madewell.com/madewell_feature/DOWELL.jsp#bjgg
[13] North Face Program:
https://www.thenorthface.com/about-us/responsibility/product/clothes-the-loop.html
[14] Patagonia: https://wornwear.patagonia.com/how-it-works

Coupon 101

I rarely pay full price for anything through combination of tactics. It's very easy to save money on any product you need by doing a few quick things!

1. Make a List

I keep a running list of things I need in the notes app on my iPhone, separated by store (grocery store, Target, etc.). I plan my shopping trips between other errands. Before I go shopping, I'll do a quick search for coupons for the things on my list. Since I've been doing this for a while, I know which brands have coupons from time to time, so it's easy now. (I've included a list of coupon websites in the next section to help!) I focus mostly on the big items like my contact solution, which normally has a $2-4 coupon.

2. Research Store Coupon Policies

Give the store a quick call or check their website before your shopping trip to save yourself time and money. The more you understand their policy, the more you can use it to your benefit.

3. Manufacturer Coupons

Large companies ranging from Johnson & Johnson to Proctor & Gamble have membership websites where you can print FREE coupons for all the products that they make. They even email you when new coupons are added! Consider using a junk mail account for these sites. They are a huge help especially for pet, health and baby items. (There's a list of coupon websites in the next section.)

4. Stack Coupons

Many retailers like Target will allow you to "stack" one manufacturer coupon with a store coupon. You can also combine this with sales in Target's Cartwheel section of their app, which lists both manufacturer coupons and Target-only discounts, that you redeem by scanning a barcode in the app at checkout.

5. Download Store Apps

Many stores allow you to collect coupons in their apps instead of cutting out paper coupons or printing them. This includes both manufacturer coupons and store-specific ones.

Many retailers offer their own loyalty programs, which are usually points systems based on how much you spend, that reward you with cash off your purchases or other savings.

For example, the Walgreens app lets me add manufacturer coupons and Walgreens coupons, which I combine with their sales. I also get a $1 worth of points each month for tracking my exercise. When they have Puffs tissues on sale for $0.99, I add the 25-cent manufacturer coupon so my tissues are only 75 cents, which—trust me—is the cheapest you'll find anywhere for that brand! I usually buy multiple boxes of Puffs and redeem the points I've collected.

6. Be Observant

We all have loyalty to certain products we love and use regularly. If you buy things regularly, chances are you know the normal price. Keep an eye out to see what stores sell it cheaper and run promotions on the item. I'm obsessed with Wheat Thins crackers, so I know how much they cost—$2.50 a box. They are normally on sale for $2 a box at most places, so I try to never pay more than that amount. When they are on sale, I buy several boxes. Both Target and HEB, my local Texas grocery store, run promotions on them regularly. Target sometimes has a better deal and I even get them for $1.25 a box!! This may seem silly, but it adds up. Let's be clear—I'm not driving to stores to check prices. If I'm in the store, I'll check for their weekly sales but that's the maximum amount of my effort.

7. Be Efficient

Driving across town in rush hour traffic to save 25 cents on produce isn't worth your time or the gas. Neither is going to the grocery store hungry without a list. I plan my shopping trips and errands together so I can make the most of my time. When I taught night classes twice a week at a university, I always stopped by Super Target on my way home at 10 p.m. It was always empty, which made shopping easier and more efficient.

8. Shop at Target

Super Target is one of the great wonders of the modern world. While Walmart might be a little cheaper, I prefer Target because the stores are nicer and the clothes fit me. Target has two wonderful things that save me money:

- **REDcard Debit Card:** Target will give you a debit card that links directly to your checking account. You get 5% off on every transaction with your card and get an extra 30 days for returns. The best part is that you get free shipping on *everything* online! I signed up for the card when I lived in Santa Barbara, California, which has no Walmart or Target but every kind of designer clothing brand you can imagine. (The town is beautiful but not functional for living on a budget.) The nearest Target was 40 miles away in Ventura, which wasn't an option with the $4 per gallon gas prices at the time, so the free shipping saved me! (They also offer a credit card with the same benefit, but the debit card is a safer option to avoid overspending.)

- **Cartwheel:** This is a coupon program built into Target's app.

When I'm in the store, I search for the things that are in my list as I'm pushing my cart down the aisles. Most of the time, most things are on sale so I just add them to my app and scan it at the checkout. Allergy meds are usually 20 percent off, which is a blessing in Austin during cedar season. (There is nothing as evil as cedar trees!)

Coupon Websites

Here is a list of coupon websites:

- **Manufacturer Websites:** Most major name brand products offer coupons directly on their website. These are often better savings than coupons from other sites listed below. Simply Google the name of the product you want to buy with the word coupon. A few websites I recommend are HealthyEssentials.com for Johnson & Johnson brands like Aveeno and Band-Aid; PgEveryday.com for Procter & Gamble brands including Tide, Dawn and Charmin; and EyeFile.com for Alcon contact solution and other eye products. Coupon values normally range from 50 cents to five dollars.

- **Coupons.com:** For the widest variety of coupons, check out this website's database of over 2,000 brands that cover a wide variety of products from Dove to Clorox cleaners. The website lets you search by category type and print coupons easily. Pro Tip: You can't search for specific brands on the site but you can search Google. For example, if you search, "Cottonelle coupon" then a link from Coupons.com will be in the top search results. This is an easy way to find specific brand coupons on the site.

- **SmartSource:** SmartSource.com is another coupon database website similar to Coupons.com. They have a smaller selection but different brands that aren't on other sites.

- **Ebates:** If you're buying something online anyways, go through Ebates.com and use their link to the store to get cash back. The percentage (1-20 percent usually) varies by retailer and the amount you earn can be directly deposited into your PayPal account. This is similar to shopping through your credit card's "shopping mall" to get extra points. I just started using this for booking my accommodation when I travel through Booking.com! You get a $10 gift card just for signing up with this referral link: *ebates.com/r/amaz812*.

- **Honey**: This browser plug-in will search the web for any coupon codes available for the websites where you shop. They also offer a cash back program. *(joinhoney.com)*

- **RetailMeNot**: A database of coupon codes for a wide variety of retailers. *(retailmenot.com)*

- **I Heart Publix**: This site contains a list of current coupons and deals at Publix grocery stores. *(iheartpublix.com)*

- **The Krazy Coupon Lady**: For an online database of coupons and weekly deals at major U.S. retailers, check out this site. *(thekrazycouponlady.com)*

- **All Things Target and Totally Target**: Both websites list weekly Target deals and coupons. *(allthignstarget.com, totallytarget.com)*

How a Super Mom Uses Coupons to Give Back to the Community

A manager at one of my previous retail jobs was a coupon ninja. Since she has a family and two kids, she really watched her spending and took advantage of couponing to an extreme but rewarding level. Back in 2009, she would get four newspapers every Sunday, clip coupons and organize them into a binder separated by section. She signed up for clubs that would mail coupons to her. This took one to three hours a week, but she has evolved to a more time efficient method with digital coupons.

The main stores she prepares to visit are BJ's, Publix and Kroger, which are grocery stores in Atlanta where she lives. She will add any applicable digital coupons on the store app the night before her trip and review the weekly deals to see what may not be on the list but a good deal. She spends less than an hour on this, and it will net a savings of at least $50 for each trip. She compiles a list of items to purchase, as well as noting whether she has a paper or digital coupon (or both) on her list to keep it organized. Simple planning saves her time while shopping, as well as making the best use of savings per trip.

Over the years, she received a ton of high-value coupons, especially for baby items, and used them to get items that were in high demand for moms living in women's shelters. This also applies to personal care items that shelters can use. She also buys pet food and treats at a discount to donate to animal shelters. Her kids even get excited and help her shop for items! This is still a very real thing that people can do to give back to their community at low or no cost, which I encourage you to try!

SECTION 3:
My Travel Hacks

When the economy tumbled in 2008, I quit everything, booked a flight to Australia, and never looked back. Recessions aren't ideal for freelance photographers. It was a bold move in uncertain times, but I gained one valuable asset—an abundance of time.

I arrived in Sydney with roughly $10,000 in my bank account, no set plans, and unlimited freedom. I found a job bartending at an old hotel with an amazing view of the opera house and started photographing bands for the Australian edition of *Rolling Stone*.

I drove the Great Ocean Road (the Australian version of the Pacific Coast Highway), hiked Kakadu National Park in Darwin and scuba dived on the Great Barrier Reef. I traveled solo or with people I met along the way.

There is a clarity that comes from traveling solo and being 5,000 miles away from everything familiar. My journey in Australia inspired a series of epic adventures that has led me to 51 countries, including a seven-month sojourn to South America in 2014-15 and my current year of globetrotting in 2018.

Traveling solo gave me the courage and confidence to build a life I wanted—not the life society wanted me to live. In hindsight, the recession was a cleverly disguised opportunity to start living my daydreams and travel for a living. This cleverly disguised opportunity is also where I learned the art of budget travel.

In this section, I discuss my travel hacking secrets:

- The Real Cost of Travel: A Budget Breakdown of my Seven-Month Latin America Trip
- Travel Banking 101
- How to Cut Costs on Top Travel Expenses
- How to Make Money While Traveling
- Where to Teach English
- The Art of Slow Travel

The Real Cost of Travel

The biggest myth about travel is that it is outrageously expensive. I bet it might even be cheaper than where you live now.

I spent seven months in Latin America and traveled to 11 countries from October 2014 until May 2015. I tracked every peso, dollar, and boliviano I spent in an expense-tracking app. Hours of analyzing the results have provided the detailed and honest breakdown of all my expenses below. (I never want to look at a spreadsheet *ever* again!) This list includes everything from pay toilets to beer!

Before any big trip, I *eliminate* my bills and focus on saving for travel. On average, I try to live on $1,000 USD a month no matter where I live. That's roughly $30/day. In Asia, this was a simple task, but I knew it was a challenge for Latin America due to high transport and visa costs in South America. Before any long-term trip, I like to have at least $10,000 in my savings account, which includes a cushion fund for when I come home. For this trip to Latin America, I saved $15,000 to help cover higher travel costs. To be clear, I have no debt.

Duration of Trip: 7 months

Total Cost of Trip: $9,714.38
Cost per Month: $1,387
Cost per Day: $46

Countries visited: 11 total including Mexico, Cuba, Costa Rica, Panama, Colombia, Argentina, Chile, Uruguay, Bolivia, Peru, and the Maldives (My friends flew me to the Maldives to photograph their amazing wedding!)

Biggest expenses: Machu Picchu ($229, which included transport from Cusco and entrance fee only), four-day Peruvian Amazon tour ($402), Torres del Paine ($246.47, including food, entrance fee, rental gear, camping and transport from Puerto Natales, Chile), Cuba ($500 for two-week trip); Bolivia Salt Flats ($179), Spanish classes ($259.30)

Summary: Overall, I stayed under my $15,000 budget and still came back to the U.S. with the cushion fund I had budgeted ($5,000). I did spend more than I hoped because I fell in love with Argentina and stayed for two months, including one month in Patagonia. Is it possible to do this trip cheaper than I did? Of course! The goal of this post is to show an *idea* of the actual cost of travel and dispel possible myths. In the end, I do not regret a thing. Every single dollar was worth it!

To view this chart in color, please visit:
http://www.travellikeanna.com/the-real-cost-of-travel

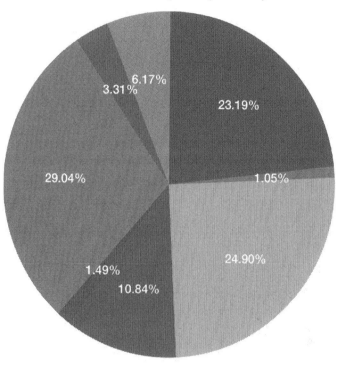

Latin America Trip Cost (7 Months)

- Accommodation - $2,252.54 (23.19%)
- Clothing/Laundry - $102.25 (1.05%)
- Food - $2,419.00 (24.90%)
- Entrance fees/Tours - $1,053.43 (10.84%)
- Toiletries/Medicine - $144.55 (1.49%)
- Transport - $2,821.02 (29.04%)
- Insurance - $321.75 (3.31%)
- Other - $599.84 (6.17%)

Detailed Breakdown of All Expenses

Accommodation: $2,252.54

I stayed in dorm beds at hostels for the majority of my trip, ranging from $8-$40 a night. I shared larger private rooms with groups of friends I met on my travels. I also rented an apartment in Buenos Aires for $35/night and split it with a friend.

Transport: $2,821.02
(Transport $2,545.22 & Visas $275.80)

- This includes every form of transport (taxis, trains, flights, ferries) and all visas.

- **Visas:** Argentina $160 reciprocity fee (*as of 2016, Americans no longer have to pay this fee*); Cuba $25; Bolivia $60 for one-month entry

- **Flights:** I flew 15 times and only paid for four flights because I'm a frequent flyer mile ninja. (This does not include the six flights to the Maldives to shoot my friend's wedding, which they paid for.) Domestic flights in Peru were only 6,000 miles each way, so I flew multiple times to save time. I booked award flights a month to six weeks in advance. My trip ended in Lima, Peru, because it is the cheapest place to fly back to the U.S. from South America. (Trust me, I did tons of research.)

- Overnight buses were my main form of transport. The buses

in Argentina were the most expensive—each bus was at least $100. I traveled only by bus and jeep from Ushuaia, the southernmost city in the world, to Cusco, Peru.

- I took an overnight ferry from Panama to Colombia for $150 because I refused to pay $350 for a one-way hour-long flight.

- There are only two ways to get to Aguas Calientes, the gateway city to Machu Picchu: take the train or walk for seven hours. I travel with 30 pounds of camera gear (and a gnome) so I gladly paid for the $150 for the scenic train.

Food: $2,419
(Eating out: $1,565.97; Groceries: $299.92; Beer: $269.99)

One of my favorite parts of traveling is the food! The older I get, the more I spend on food. I eat well and never eat ramen, but I do eat a lot of peanut butter. Usually, I make peanut butter, banana and honey sandwiches for long bus rides or transit days when food options are limited. (*TIP: Always pack a jar of natural peanut butter before a trip – it's either hard to find or expensive overseas.*)

I ate my weight in steak and fresh berries in Argentina, all of which were extremely cheap. I cooked a lot in hostels with other travelers, which meant most meals only cost about a few dollars. I also tried to only stay at places with free breakfast.

I only spent $13.12 on water because I took a Sawyer MINI water filter with me, which saved a lot of money and plastic.

The tap water was drinkable in Argentina, Southern Chile, Panama, and certain parts of both Colombia and Costa Rica.

Entrance Fees/Tours: $1,053.43

This includes all museums, archeological sites, hiking, and admission to national parks and cultural attractions like Machu Picchu ($40); four-day Amazon tour in Iquitos, Peru ($403.91); Torres del Paine admission ($30); and Bolivia salt flats tour ($179)

Toiletries/Medicine: $144.55
(Toiletries: $54.39; Medical: $90.16)

This includes shampoo, over-the-counter medicines like ibuprofen, toothpaste, and bandages for when I smashed my knees (and my iPhone) on a morning run in a park in Buenos Aires.

Contact solution was $20 in Panama! When possible, I *always* buy sunscreen and contact solution in the U.S. before I leave because it's either hard to find, poor quality, or overpriced abroad.

Clothing/Laundry: $102.25
(Clothing: $45.83; Laundry $56.42)

The only clothing items I really bought were socks and a llama sweater and gloves for Bolivia and Peru. I usually only pack for summer because I hate the cold. It's easier and cheaper to just buy a llama sweater, gloves and socks than drag warm clothing around for five months.

Insurance: $321.75

I paid $50/month for zero-deductible travel medicine insurance with emergency evacuation coverage and an adventure sports rider through IMGlobal. I opted for the 30 days of home coverage after I returned to give me time to sort out my American insurance. (They no longer offer home coverage in the U.S. as option.) I always cancel my American health insurance when I travel long-term because most U.S. policies offer only limited international coverage.

Other Expenses: $599.84

This includes the following: pay toilets ($3.91), gifts ($34.65), postage ($56.92), Spanish classes ($259.30),; WiFi ($16.42), tips ($36.17); other ($192.47).

Travel Banking 101

The easiest way to save money while traveling is having the right kind of bank accounts. There are two big fees that add up when using your debit and credit cards abroad.

1. Foreign Transaction Fees

Most banks and credit cards charge a small fee to convert the currency ranging from one to three percent.

2. ATM fees

Banks will also charge you a fee for using a non-partner ATM abroad. Plus, the ATM you use abroad will most likely charge you a fee as well. That can be as much as $15 per ATM withdrawal! That's six meals at the street market in Thailand!

How to Avoid Bank Fees

1. Find a free, no-fee bank account

The Charles Schwab Investor Checking Account is the greatest thing since the invention of the burrito. No minimum balance. No ATM fees. No foreign transaction fees. They also refund any ATM fee charged to you by another bank at the end of every month. (They just refunded $37 in ATM fees to me last month!) They also have 24-hour customer service, and they are seriously nicest people ever. You can call them toll-free in the U.S. From abroad, Skype allows you to call toll-free numbers for no fee from overseas

This is a free account, so it can be used solely as a travel account or as your main account. I opened two accounts with them in case one card was lost or stolen. That way I can transfer money from one account to the other without any issues. It's also my main checking account.

For more information on free, no-fee checking accounts, check out NerdWallet.com. I have no affiliation to them, but find their site to be a good resource for banking. They offer charts and lists of the top rated accounts.

2. Use Partner Banks

If you want to keep your current bank, research their partner banks abroad. Both the ATM free and the foreign transaction fee or either could be waived or lowered. Outside of Europe and Australia, there aren't many options if you use U.S.-based banks.

3. Look for ATMs that don't charge fees.

Most ATMs in India and Mongolia don't charge a fee. Avoid well-known worldwide bank ATMs like Citibank or HSBC because they *always* charge a high fee. Use local banks instead. They might still charge a fee, but it will be less than a mainstream bank.

4. Credit Unions

Local credit union accounts might also help you avoid fees. ATM fees might still be an issue but are usually lower at credit unions. Foreign transaction fees will be less of an issue as well. Check with them in advance before any travel to confirm rates.

5. No-Fee Credit Cards

There is no foreign transaction fee for any Capital One credit card. Many airline cards and Chase are following suit. Keep in mind that some rewards cards, like the Chase Sapphire Reserve, have annual fees but no foreign transaction fees. Bottom line: Only use cards with no foreign transaction fees. There are also many rewards credit cards without an annual fee that waive foreign transaction fees.

What Type of Credit Card is Best for Travel?

Ideally, you shouldn't pay more than one credit card annual fee a year even if you are a frequent traveler. It's also easier to maximize your points if you only use one card for all of your spending. I recommend at least having another card with no annual fee to use as a backup in case one doesn't work while traveling, which is very common abroad.

Rewards Credit Cards

If you are going to have a credit card, you should be earning rewards of some kind. The best travel card on the market right now is the Chase Sapphire Reserve, which offers 3 points per dollar spent on travel and food. They also offer a 1.5-point ratio when redeeming for travel. You also get free Global Entry ($100 value) every five years. The fee is hefty ($450/year), *but* you get a $300 credit for travel expenses during the year, which brings the fee down to $150 a year. It's technically only $50 the first year *if* you get Global Entry. You also get Priority Pass, which is a $100 value and gives you access to airport lounges worldwide. (Both Global Entry and Priority Pass are life-changing!)

If you spend $4,000 in the first three months, you get a 50,000-mile bonus worth $750 in free travel! Another perk for the card is you can redeem miles for a partial cost of travel and pay the rest.

Is it worth the fee? If you travel a lot, then yes. For me, it's been the perfect card. If you don't travel a lot, then consider the lower-tier Chase Sapphire with only a $95 fee (waived the first year) and two points per dollar on travel/dining.

Keep in mind that when you redeem credit card miles for travel, you can still earn frequent flyer miles on those flights. Don't forget to add your frequent flyer number to the reservation!

Check out NerdWallet.com for more options. They have a great list of the best travel rewards card on the market. The highest rated travel rewards card with no annual fee is the Bank of America Travel Rewards Card, which offers 1.5 points per dollar spent.

Rewards credit cards are only beneficial if you can meet the purchase requirements for the initial opening bonus with your normal spending habits. Do not get a rewards card if you can't pay off the balance every month or have to overspend to reach the limit. If you open multiple cards, consider using a free credit monitoring service like CreditKarma.com to monitor your credit and check your score.

Airline Cards

If you are loyal to a specific airline, then airlines cards are worth it. I also have the American Airlines card, which gives me free checked bags on all flights and priority boarding. These cards are now starting to offer no foreign transaction fees! Since the airlines revamped their reward structures over the past few years, I find that I often need to fly airlines that aren't my preferred airline, so this card isn't as valuable to me personally partly since I now live closer to a United hub than American Airlines.

Eight Essential Travel Banking Tips

1. **Plan ahead.** Open any new bank accounts three months before you leave for your trip. This eliminates any hassles with holds on funds that occur on new accounts.

2. **Ask about fees.** Some banks charge a monthly maintenance fee if you don't keep a large daily balance or have a monthly direct deposit. Check with your bank in advance if you will be traveling long-term without any direct deposits. This was a huge issue for me and the reason I closed both my Bank of America and Wells Fargo accounts. Be sure to also ask about foreign transaction fees and alert your bank to your travel plans so they don't block your cards.

3. **Take multiple cards.** I always travel with a Visa, MasterCard, and American Express. Visa and MasterCard are the most universally accepted cards, although I find American Express can work better on some airline websites abroad like Qantas. But beware—despite their catchy slogan, American Express is *not* everywhere you want them to be. They were not in Cambodia. They left me stranded and living in Western Union commercial calling my parent's at 5 a.m. to transfer me money.

4. **Keep an eye on exchange rates.** If your home currency looks like it's dropping, then take out cash before it gets worse. If your home currency spikes, hit up the ATM! When I lived in Australia, there were a few weeks when the Australian dollar dipped low. I took out a good chunk of money out of my U.S. accounts and deposited it into my Australian account.

5. **Avoid exchanging currency at airports.** You will get the worst rates. You are better using an ATM. The only exceptions are countries like Burma or Vietnam, where you get better exchange rates with cash on the black market.

6. **Always take U.S. dollars.** No matter the currency, many places will accept U.S. dollars as payment as well. Ask for prices in both the local currency and U.S. to compare. For example, I saved $9 paying in USD for the Easter Island park entry fee but saved $54 paying for my six-night accommodation on the island in local currency. Larger bills often get the best exchange rates but keep some smaller cash handy as well.

7. **Find proper ATMs.** If the ATM is in a strange place, like a hotel lobby or in a sketchy corner of a convenience store, it probably has higher ATM fees and the worst exchange rates. Go to a proper bank ATM.

8. **Pay in Local Currency.** Many shops will give you the option to pay in your home currency (or USD), but the rate is 5 percent higher! (Trust me, I did the math!) Always pay in local currency in shops that give you the option to do both. I had no choice but to pay in Euro for my rental car in Iceland, which worked out in my favor since I booked far in advance. The rate dropped so I saved about $25 when I paid upon arrival! Sometimes, the USD rate can save you money. Download the free XE currency exchange app first to check rates before deciding.

High-Yield Savings Accounts

If you currently don't have a savings account or method for investing money, consider a high-yield savings account, which offers a high annual-percentage rate with no fees or minimums. I'm a big fan of the Barclay's High-Yield Savings account. This online-only account currently offers 1.9 percent APR with no minimums or fees. (Most bank savings accounts only pay .01 percent interest.) This is one of the best on the market currently. This is excellent way to start saving money or to use if you need to access the money frequently while traveling.

This account isn't the best method for long-term investing or saving for retirement. Consider reading books by Dave Ramsey or Tony Robbins for more on investing.

Like all savings accounts, you are limited to six transfers a month, according to government regulation. It takes a few days to transfer money, but is very efficient. I've been using it for the past two years and I love it! (FYI: I have no affiliation with Barclay's.)

How to Cut Costs on Top Travel Expenses

Accommodation, food, and transport are the top three expenses in life and travel. I've compiled a list of ways to cut costs on all three while traveling. Get out of your comfort zone and go see the world!

How to Save on Accommodation

Reduce Hotel Rates

If the thought of staying in a hostel makes you shiver, here's a few tips to cut back on hotel costs and maximize your value:

- **Call hotel directly.** Instead of calling the 1-800 number, call the hotel directly to get a more personalized experience with a better chance of a free upgrade.

- **Use membership discounts.** Most hotels offer AAA and AARP rates that are at least 10 percent cheaper than regular rates. I use this all the time with my AAA discount.

- **Loyalty Programs.** For every 10 nights you book on Hotels.com, you get one free. Sign up for hotel specific loyalty programs as well that offer free upgrades, Wi-Fi, and other deals. Hotels.com and Hotwire.com both give you discounts for signing up for their free loyalty program. Booking.com offers a discount of 10 percent on select properties if you book five stays in less than two years. (I used this a lot in South America for all types of accommodation.)

- **Price drop alerts.** Both Hotels.com and Kayak.com have the option to sign up for alerts when hotel prices drop.

- **Book last minute.** Apps like Hotel Tonight offer last minute deals, while Hotwire lets you book a hotel based on the location area for a deal. You find out the name of the property only after booking.

- **Get the right credit card.** The Citi Prestige card gives you the fourth night free for consecutive night stays at the same hotel. My friend Linda swears by this card because it saved her $1,000 last year. While the fee is hefty ($450), this is offset by the $250 annual travel credit, free yearly Priority Pass lounge access ($100 value) and free Global Entry ($100 every five years). If you travel frequently and will only stay in hotels, this is good value. I rarely use hotels, so it's not worth it for me.

- **Referrals.** Booking.com will give you $25 credit on your credit card for each friend you refer to the website that makes a $50 or higher booking. Your friend gets the same bonus. I've referred several of my friends on my current trip! Rewards programs like Marriott's will give you up to 50,000 bonus points for referring friends.

Types of Budget Accommodation

Airbnb

Chances are you've already used Airbnb. The concept is simple: people rent out rooms and couches in their homes for a fee. They post profiles about the space and guests provide reviews. Airbnb verifies the identity of all hosts, offers a secure payment platform, insurance and 24/7 customer service. It's a great option for locations without hostels. Be sure to have a friend refer you and offer a reference.

When I lived in California, my roommate and I rented out the IKEA futon in our living room for $75/night and met some cool folks. I booked a nice room in Cartagena for $40/night that I'll spilt with a friend for our trip in April, which is honestly cheaper than a hotel *and* a hostel. It's a great experience and cost effective.

Camping

When I travel in the U.S., I camp almost 90 percent of the time to cut back on costs. I stay mostly at KOA (Kampgrounds of America) campgrounds or campgrounds in national parks, which cost roughly $15-35/night. This price is even lower when I split it between the people I'm traveling with. Every KOA I've stayed at has been extremely nice with spotless bathrooms and WiFi! (My favorite is in Santa Fe!)

Couchsurfing

This is simple: It's just like Airbnb, except people let you crash on their couch for *free*. Reviews are the heart of this experience. Be sure to have friends provide references for you when you sign up initially. For safety concerns, check out the safety section of their website. If 80 people say a person is cool, then odds are they are actually cool.

The website is also a great community for meetups and events, including language groups and social activities. When I moved to California, I couchsurfed while I was looking for a place to live and made a cool friend who's also a big traveler.

Hostels

Hostels are the best place to meet other travelers. You essentially rent out a bed in a dorm of 3-20 people. They feature shared showers and lockers for your valuables. (Pack your shower shoes and a sturdy lock.) Private rooms and female-only dorms are also available. Most have full kitchens and some offer free breakfast. It's basically like being in college again without having to go to class. Prices range from $6 (in Asia and Central America) to $50 (NYC and Japan).

You can find hostels and reviews on Booking.com, Trip Advisor and HostelWorld. To avoid booking fees, book with the hostel directly. If you are planning a long stay, only pay for the first couple nights when you arrive to make sure you like the place. I personally use Booking.com with an Ebates.com referral link to earn a commission on my booking. If the price is cheaper elsewhere, Booking.com will match it!

House Sitting/Pet Sitting

I am the official house/pet sitter for Austin, Texas. Handsome chatty parrots that say "What's for breakfast?", fluffy cats named Adam, and overly energetic dogs are my specialty. My roommate's lease ended a few months before I left for my 2014 Latin America trip. Conveniently, several friends needed house/pet sitters while I was homeless. It was a win-win situation for everyone.

It's a good way to save on rent before your travels and find free accommodation on the road. My friend, Carla, spent several months house sitting when she moved to Australia. Make sure you leave the house better than you found it.

Here are two great resources for finding house/pet sitting gigs: Trustedhousesitters.com ($119 annual fee) and Mindmyhouse.com ($20 annual fee).

Stay with Friends or Friends of Friends

The more you travel, the more your traveling network expands. Your friends also have friends. Ask around before your trip or put a post on Facebook to see if anyone is in your destination.

I am eternally grateful for all the people who have let me crash on their couches. They've been an essential part of my traveling experience. Before this trip, I did a two-week Amtrak trip through the East Coast and stayed with friends the entire trip except one night in Vermont. When I moved to Australia, I emailed a lady I met at a wedding about grabbing lunch after I got to Sydney. She instantly offered to let me stay with her family until I found a place to live. The kindness of others is astounding.

Most people will offer you a place to stay instantly. If I ask, I always make a point to say, "If that's not a convenient time, then I completely understand." That gives them the option to be honest if the timing is not good, and there are no hard feelings. I always make a point of leaving handmade cards for people who let me crash at their place. Or I buy them beer/wine and add them to my postcard list.

Don't forget karma. Offer your couch to friends and friends of friends. Sign up for Couchsurfing.

Five Essential Accommodation Tips

1. Be Aware of High and Low Seasons.

Costs can triple during holidays and high seasons. Book in advance. Be aware of national holidays in your destination country. It's easier to negotiate prices in the low season, but the weather might not be ideal. Guidebooks provide a good breakdown for seasons and holidays on their first few pages or a quick Google search will yield the same results. Christmas, New Year's and Easter are always peak seasons. During the low season, I lived well on $15/day in Khao Lak, a beach town north of Phuket in Southern Thailand. That's cheaper than any place I've lived in the States.

2. Skip the A/C

Air conditioning isn't standard outside of the U.S. Opting for a room with a fan or with cold water only will cut the price significantly. Plus, you really should be spending more time exploring than sitting in your room! Trust me, you don't need warm water in the tropics. Sometimes, it's not even an option!

3. Pay in Local Currency

Whether you are paying online or in person, it's almost always cheaper to pay in local currency. Currency conversion rates are usually inflated for profit. Sometimes, it helps to check the exchange rate just to be safe. I'm renting a room with a friend in Easter Island in March is $50 USD/night or 25,000

Chilean pesos, which is $41.85 USD with the current exchange rate. I'm clearly paying in pesos.

4. Share a Room with Friends

Private rooms in hostels are usually the same cost per person as a dorm bed or cheaper. Guesthouses are another great option. They have fewer facilities than a hotel but offer private rooms with private baths.

I shared a three-bed room in a guesthouse with three friends in Laos a few years back for $4 per night *each*. That included an amazing private balcony, private bathroom, air conditioning and free Wi-Fi. Seriously. Traveling can be cheaper than you think.

5. Pay in Advance

If your dates are set, paying in advance online can save you 10 percent at least when booking directly through the accommodation. Websites like Booking.com can also have cheaper rates as well for advance bookings.

How to Eat for Cheap

Food is my biggest expense. I will pay $4 for my accommodation and spend $15 on breakfast. I like to eat. Luckily fresh, quality food can be significantly cheaper abroad because the produce is local and not shipped across the world.

Eat with the Locals

If a restaurant is full of foreigners, it's not going to be cheap. Street food and local restaurants offer the best quality food at the cheapest prices. A meal at a street market in Thailand will only cost a couple dollars. You can get a street quesadilla for $1.50 in Mexico. Most local markets have a section of vendors serving prepared meals. Follow the crowds of locals. (Street food is pretty much safe, though be careful in India. I speak from experience.) Ask your hostel or accommodation for suggestions of great places where they—not the tourists—eat.

Food Courts

All the big fancy malls in Bangkok have amazing food courts with delicious and cheap food stalls with dishes less than $2. Avoid the proper restaurants that surround the food court. Even ritzy Singapore has large hawker centers where you can get a meal for less than $5 and fresh juice for $1.50.

Skip the Soda

Drink water or fresh juice. It's cheaper and healthier than a soda. Fresh squeezed juice is roughly $1/glass in Asia and Latin America. I mentioned previously that the two different student travel companies I worked for did not allow students to buy drinks with meals. They only provided water. Bottom line: Drinks are expensive.

Pack a Water Filter

I'm THAT girl. The one who's filtering the water in the Cancun airport bathroom because she refused to pay $3 for a tiny plastic bottle of water. Buy a water filter and filter your own instead of wasting money on plastic bottles, which are bad for the environment. As I mentioned previously, I recommend the Sawyer MINI Filter. It's tiny, inexpensive ($20) and easy to use. I've been using it for the past four months in Central and South America. Also, invest in a good insulated reusable water bottle like Klean Kanteen. Avoid anything that's not BPA-free or aluminum. Stainless steel is easy to sanitize with hot water and keeps beverages colder longer. Both the water bottle and filter will save you a fortune in airports!

Free Breakfast

Look for accommodation that includes free breakfast. Be sure to inquire about the type of free breakfast. I just emailed two hostels in Medellin, Colombia, asking what they offer for breakfast. The one with the best breakfast gets my business. Check reviews—if the breakfast is bad, it will be noted.

Cook

Most Airbnb options and hostels have full kitchens. I cooked dinner every night for a week in Oaxaca, Mexico, with some new friends from my hostel. We each spent $2/night on food at the local market. We had quality, hearty meals filled with tons of local, fresh vegetables and even homemade tortillas from the street market. The best thing about traveling is that you can buy produce and eggs individually, so it's easy to buy exactly what you need!

Peanut Butter

Nothing will get you through long bus rides or early mornings like peanut butter. Food at train and bus stations is usually overpriced and horrible. It's also notorious for causing food poisoning. Make a peanut butter sandwich for the road and treat yourself to a good dinner when you arrive. Buy a jar of natural peanut butter before you leave home at Trader Joe's or Whole Foods for $3. (By natural, I mean unsalted and no artificial sweeteners.) Grab some local honey and bananas at the street market for a real treat. I'll grab bread from a local bakery and make sandwiches on the train. Skip the boxed ramen—it's gross and bad for you.

Don't Skimp on the Tip

Traveling on a budget isn't an excuse to be cheap. Consider gratuities in your budget when eating out and tip according to local customs. Guidebooks will give you a good idea of what is appropriate for local customs in restaurants versus taxis, etc.

Bartending and waiting tables funded a great deal of my travels. Tipping is heavily relied on for survival in many parts of the world, especially when non-democratic governments are involved.

How to Cut Costs on Transport

Use Public Transport

Most large cities have efficient and affordable large-scale train or bus networks connecting the airport with the city center. (Even Delhi has a great air-conditioned metro train system.) Take a local bus instead of a taxi to the bus/train station or airport for one-tenth of the price. Daily and weekly passes are a good deal if you travel frequently. (*Always* get the seven-day pass in NYC.)

Many parts of the world have a system of pickup trucks with seats in the back that have routes just like buses. They will drop you anywhere for next to nothing. In Thailand, they are called songthaews. Take advantage of them!

Night Buses and Trains

Night buses and trains are my favorite form of transport. For long journeys, both help save time and accommodation costs. Most overnight trains include options for beds. The sleeper trains in Thailand, Spain, and India are pretty comfy and affordable. Plus, you don't waste a day traveling. Aside from specific areas of Central and South America, night transportation is extremely safe. Even in those locations, it's safe if you travel with private, reputable companies.

Rail Passes

England, mainland Europe, Australia and Japan have great rail pass options for travelers and students. Check prices of individual tickets to see if it's worth it for your planned route. Plan in advance because most rail passes have to be purchased *before* you leave your home country. Students receive a significant discount on passes so take advantage!

Local Buses

VIP Tourist buses are an overpriced scam with blaring TVs and are often a target for thieves. Most countries have cheaper, comfy local buses for half the price. In Thailand, I always take first-class buses for half the cost. They still include large comfy seats, air conditioning, a bathroom, and a free bottle of water/meal. There are even cheaper open-air "chicken" buses. These can be rough for long trips but are great for short day trips. These are completely safe in Southeast Asia, but women traveling alone should be cautious in other parts of the world.

South America has some pretty swanky bus options, which can run $50-100 for a 16- to 36-hour bus ride. This is cheaper than flying and worth the money for the comfort.

Taxis and Tuk Tuks

Agree on a price in advance, or ask to use the meter. Ask locals the fair/standard price for your route beforehand then negotiate accordingly.

Be sure to compare costs. Tuk tuks are a great deal in India but outrageous in Thailand. A metered air-conditioned taxi will be a one-fourth of the cost in Bangkok. Taxi fares increase during rush hour, late at night, and for airport routes. Drivers might also charge exorbitant flat rates on weekends and near tourist spots. Sometimes it's best to negotiate a taxi to the nearest public transport station instead of your final destination, then take a train or bus.

Research reputable taxi companies in countries with safety concerns. In India, I only use Meru or a private taxi provided by my hotel. In Bogota, I use the Tappsi app for safe taxis.

Flights

- **Research local budget airlines**. They don't always show up in big travel search engines especially Southwest. (I find Kayak.com and Skyscanner.com are the best search engines with the best deals and airline options.) Book with the airline directly if possible.

- **Consider flying to the closest major city to your destination.** Then, take public transport or a budget airline flight. I always take a bus/train combo to Southern Thailand from Bangkok to save flight costs.

- **Check for luggage fees and pay them in advance.** Some budget airlines increase baggage fees significantly on the day of the flight and charge heavily for overage. Print your boarding pass because some also charge if you don't!

- **Research airport public transit.** If a city has several airports, consider transportation costs to the city from both airports. Budget airlines can fly into the smaller, domestic airports with less transport options.

- **Fly into smaller airports.** In the U.S. consider flying into smaller airports to save money. Flights to Columbia, South Carolina, are sometimes cheaper than Charlotte and have better connection options. Since my parents live between both cities, I choose what's the cheapest when I visit them.

- **Be aware of arrival times.** Is affordable, safe transport available at 3 a.m.? It's better to sleep in the airport for a few hours and catch the first train into the city than fork out a fortune for a taxi in the middle of the night in a strange city. It also saves accommodation costs. Considering paying a little extra to fly in at a more reasonable time if transport is outrageous during the night.

- **Keep track of your frequent flyer miles.** Sign up for the frequent flyer mile programs for the major airlines in your country/area. Most major airlines are part of global alliances allowing you to earn miles on another carrier's flights. I fly at least once a year on miles.

- **Avoid government-owned airlines.** Government-owned airlines in third-world countries are notorious for being unreliable and can have sketchy safety records. Do your research. Foreign-owned airlines are usually nicer, safe and more reliable. (Indigo is my favorite budget airline in India, and they fly to other parts of Asia as well. Interjet is the best in Mexico and Central America. Both are super nice!).

General Transportation Tips

1. Buy Tickets in Advance

Purchase tickets directly at the stations. Travel agencies, hotels, and hostels add commission. Prices can be significantly lower in advance. You also get first choice for seats, which is ideal if you are prone to motion sickness. (The front row on the right side usually has the most legroom on buses.) When you arrive in a city at a station, consider buying your departure ticket before you leave the station.

2. Get it in Writing

If you change a ticket, *always* do it in person and get it in writing. Always get a printed copy of any ticket. If you only get a receipt, be sure to have the contact info for the person you bought it from if an issue arises.

3. Consider Transport Options

When deciding between different forms of transport, factor in the cost and difficulty of getting from the airport or station to your final destination. Your arrival time will be the main factor. Consider the total cost of getting to your accommodation, not just the cost of getting to the city.

4. Ride Shares

Share rides with other travelers to airports or border crossings. Make friends and ask their final destination. Ask local travel agents for available ride shares and compare with taxi rates. Sometimes it's a better deal and less hassle to go with a travel agent. Uber and similar apps are available in most big cities across the world and significantly cheaper than standard transit rates.

5. Skip Airport Taxi Surcharges

Grab a taxi at the departures hall in the airport to avoid paying the extra airport taxi fee at arrivals. The minute someone gets out of a taxi, I ask the driver if I can have a ride. (This worked well for me at Bangkok's main airport, Suvarnabhumi, and saved a ton of time.)

6. Take a Boat

Ferries are totally reliable method of transport and a fraction of the cost of flying. I recently took a ferry from Panama to Colombia. There's no land crossing between the two countries due to political unrest and jungle terrain. Flying from Panama City to Cartagena was close to $370 *one-way* for a 45-minute flight. (This is ridiculous considering a friend flew one-way from San Francisco to Cartagena to meet me for less than $300!) The 18-hour ferry was $150 for a private cabin and $100 for a seat. (I did the cabin.) Considering I'm technically unemployed and living on my savings, I figured 18 hours of my time was worth saving the $200. Plus, I got a ton of work and reading done, and I met some new amazing friends!

In coastal towns, water taxis and boats are the best and fastest option. Negotiation is key. Ask people at the port if they are going the same area to help reduce the cost for everyone.

7. Take Advantage of Free Ride Promos

Sign up for mobile taxi services with Uber and Lyft. You get an instant monetary credit for your first ride and additional credits for each person you refer. Refer anyone traveling with you so you both benefit with all the free rides. You'd be surprised how many cities in the world use both services! Many places also have similar rideshare apps like Grab in Southeast Asia.

8. Walk

Book accommodation that's centrally located to things you want to do or is close to public transport to save on transit costs.

How to Make Money While Traveling

Whether you're looking to move abroad completely or go for a short stint, there are multiple ways to make money while traveling. The easiest answer is to freelance. Over half of the U.S. workforce is expected to be freelance in the next 10 years, according to a 2017 study by Upwork and the Freelancer's Union.

1. Work Remotely at Your Current Job

This is the easiest option: keep your current job and work remotely! Give it some thought, make a list of concerns and find solutions to each. Approach your boss and discuss options. Offer to come back a few times a year if needed for big events and meetings. Consider joining a program like Remote Year (*remoteyear.com*) and Wifi Tribe (*wifitribe.co*) that brings together professionals who work remotely into a community that travels together. These aren't cheap but have big perks.

2. Be a Tour Guide

I ran photo trips for high school students in Asia for five summers, which was one of the most amazing jobs I've ever had. I ran a similar trip in Yellowstone National Park last summer for another company. I love teaching people about traveling and photography. If you are interested in similar actives, research companies that offer trips that cater to your area of interest or expertise: yoga, hiking, marine biology, etc. If you relocate to another place, you can even start running your own specialty tours on Airbnb Experiences. (My friends just did a coffee tour in Buenos Aires last week!) These types of jobs usually cover all of your travel expenses, which significantly decreases your cost of living since food and accommodation are provided. This is part of how I traveled for so long on such a small budget.

3. Apply for a Working Holiday Visa

I lived in Australia for almost a year on a Working Holiday Visa. These types of visas allow 18- to 30-year-olds to work while they travel. I worked a few random bar jobs and also photographed bands for *Rolling Stone* magazine. Pretty random, I know, but the options are endless.

Australia and New Zealand offer one-year visas for Americans and many other nationalities aged 18-30, which allow you to work anywhere. They cost roughly $320 and $165 respectively for the visas depending on exchange rate when you book.

For students or recent graduates, there are similar visa

programs in South Korea ($45USD fee), Canada ($200 USD), Singapore ($150 USD fee) and Ireland ($300 USD fee). You must do these programs within 12 months of graduating. The website GoOverseas.com has a great guide for Working Holiday programs for Americans. Check out the Working Abroad post on my blog, TravelLikeAnna.com for more information.

4. Teach English

Teaching English is a great way to live abroad and fund your travels. I taught English in Thailand briefly and seriously considered similar opportunities in Korea and Japan. A Bachelor's degree is required or preferred by many programs. Most programs prefer that you don't speak the native language. A TEFL (Teaching English as a Foreign Language) or TESOL (Teaching English as a Second Language) certificate is not required for the programs listed below but can increase your salary. (FYI: I don't have either certification. Private schools usually require it.) The highest paid programs are in Japan and Korea. Visas are almost always provided by employers.

The most established and highest-paid programs provide the most training. Otherwise, be prepared to improvise. Be aware that many programs do not follow the traditional American or British school calendars for holidays (i.e., no Christmas break). Please refer to the next section about where to teach English for a list of options and resources.

5. Teach at an International School

If you have the qualifications to teach in the U.S., you can teach abroad at an international school in a wide variety of subjects. Many international schools are part of the International Baccalaureate (IB) program and want teachers who have experience in the program.

6. Teach Online (Consulting/Tutoring)

No matter your skill set, there's someone out there who would like to learn from you. There's several platforms that allow you to teach everything online, from search engine optimization to finance. Here are a few examples: Clarity.fm, Tutor.com, Takelessons.com and Teachable.com.

7. Be a Flight Attendant

Getting paid to travel is the ultimate goal. There's no better way than as a flight attendant! Keep in mind that even working for an airline in any capacity often means you travel for free! I have friends who work part-time jobs at the airport just for this benefit.

8. Try Your Hand at Day Trading

If you have the finance background or want to invest the time to learn, you can make money in the stock market. While it can be risky, the rewards can be worth it. I'm currently traveling with a friend who dabbles in day trading and has been growing her retirement account significantly!

9. Explore Digital Media Opportunities

Most digital media fields (graphic/web design, social media, SEO, marketing, etc.) can be done remotely. Take your business on the road. It's very rare that these types of work require you to be physically present in the same location as a client. If you need to chat, schedule a Skype or FaceTime call. Websites like Upwork allow you to find clients easily and for them to find you. Forbes[15] also has a great article that lists 79 websites for getting freelance work. Check with creative staffing agencies in your hometown to see what local opportunities are available.

10. Travel Nursing & Healthcare Providers

If you are a nurse, doctor or other type of medical professional, you can work across the U.S. and abroad in a variety of short-term positions that range from weeks to years depending on the location. The more remote the location, the higher the pay (specialty units also usually command higher rates, e.g., ICUs, Pediatric ICU, etc.). For example, positions in the Middle East can pay two or three times normal salaries and are often tax free.

---

[15] https://www.forbes.com/sites/abdullahimuhammed/2017/06/16/79-websites-to-get-freelance-jobs-fast/#52bd69b71688

For U.S.-based positions, the real money is in the housing and food stipends. Both are tax free as long as you are a certain distance from your actual "home." The travel nurses that I've met recommend finding your own housing and taking advantage of both stipends instead of using the housing provided by the travel agency. This ties in with making the most of your work benefits, which I discussed earlier in the book. Advanced planning is a must for travel nursing since paperwork can take a while. For more information, check out nursing blogs[16] or seek out colleagues with experience.

11. Be a Scuba/Surfing/Yoga/Dance Instructor

When I was in Southern Thailand, I noticed that almost all of the scuba instructors were from South Africa. I've been taking tango classes in Buenos Aires the last two weeks, and the majority of the instructors aren't locals either. If you have a specific skill, then reach out to places that offer that service. Worst case scenario: you could always work for free room and board!

12. Work on Cruise Ships

I have several friends who work as photography instructors on cruise ships. It's a great way for them to travel for free and still be paid. Even if you aren't a photographer, you can find a job on a ship that matches your skill set. My doctor once

---

[16]https://travelnursingblogs.com/travel-nursing-resource-guide/travel-nursing-websites/

confided in me that she regrets not taking a job as doctor on a cruise ship. Check out AllCruiseJobs.com for postings!

13. Rent Out Your House

If you plan on being on the road for a while, rent out your place to cover travel costs and increase your savings. (I don't believe in paying rent for a place I'm not living in!) Get a friend or family member to manage it while you are away.

14. Try Drop Shipping

Essentially, drop shipping is a fulfillment service where a company sells things online which are shipped directly from the manufacturer to the customer. They never touch the product or have any inventory. Usually, this requires a very niche market. You can't just sell bicycles, you have to sell mountain bike accessories. There are courses and plenty of resources on the internet like DropshipLifestyle.com. I have no experience with this but a lot of people do this to fund their travels.

15. Be a Social Media Influencer

If you have a large following—over 10,000—on Instagram and other social media platforms, you can be paid to promote a wide variety of products to your audience. You probably follow some of these people on Instagram. One day they are staying in some fancy hotel, the next they are selling jewelry and the next day they are selling pasta. High-level influencers can make close to $10,000 per post, from what I've read in interviews.

While many influencers get free things (clothing, hotels, etc.), they still might not be making money. I personally don't follow this route because it feels inauthentic to me. Why would I promote a fancy hotel I couldn't afford to stay in myself? Ethically, I don't accept free or press trips, but this is how some people make a living or subsidize their travels.

I'm not trying to discourage you from following this route but want to offer two bits of advice: be honest about sponsorships/paid content and make sure you are actually getting *paid* for your work, not just getting free things. You can't buy tacos with free hotel nights. Tacos are important.

16. Write an eBook

If you have an expert in a certain field, you can self-publish an eBook and put it on Amazon. It's an excellent way to make passive income. One of my friends put his college thesis on Amazon and did very little marketing. He sold a few thousand dollars' worth in the first six months and still sells some occasionally. Imagine what you can do if you if you put in some effort! Pat Flynn from SmartPassiveIncome.com has a great free eBook on how to write an eBook.

17. Start a blog

There are many ways to make money off a blog: sell products, eBooks, courses, advertising, sponsored posts, etc. The more niche your blog is, the better. Instead of writing about bass fishing, focus on kayak bass fishing. (Yes, this is a thing!) The main goal of my blog is to provide value to my readers, which should be the purpose of every blog. There's no point in starting a blog if it's not providing value to others.

18. Affiliate Marketing

Affiliate marketing is a great way to make passive income but can be difficult. Essentially, you promote another person's product in exchange for a referral fee. This works best if you have a pre-existing platform to promote these products. You should only promote products you love and be clear that you are including affiliate links. Amazon Affiliates is a very popular one. If someone buys anything off Amazon after clicking on your link, then you get a small percentage at no cost to them. I used Amazon affiliates in blog posts where I talk about packing but have made less than $40 in two years. This is for two reasons: my content isn't ripe for tons of affiliate links, which only go well in certain posts, and I only post links when relevant.

19. Work in Hotels or Hostels

Working in both hotels and hostels are great ways to travel and get discount rates on accommodation. There are a variety of positions on websites like HotelJobs.com that range from managers to cooks to engineers.

20. Consider Work Exchange Programs

Work Exchange programs are a great way to volunteer your time in exchange for room and board. Many companies link hosts with volunteers. The time frame can range from days to months. There is no age requirement, and it's also possible to volunteer as a family with children.[17] I've met many people during my travels who have used the programs below.

- **WWOOF** specializes with opportunities on organic farms across the world. *(wwoof.net)*

- **WorkAway** offers a variety of options including positions in schools, cafes, hostels and farms. Membership costs $38 USD per year. (I stayed at many amazing hostels run by WorkAway staff!) *(workaway.info)*

- **HelpX** is an alternative to WorkAway that provides positions at hostels, ranches, and many other options. It's free to sign up but costs 20 Euros for the two-year premier membership. *(helpx.net)*

21. Be a House or Pet Sitter

Another great option is to house and pet sit. While some of these opportunities pay, others simply offer free accommodation. There are several websites that match homeowners with sitters. Most charge an annual fee to access the site: TrustedHousesitters.com and MindMyHouse.com.

---

[17] http://wwoof.net/post/wwoofing-with-a-toddler-successfully

22. Join the Peace Corps

The Peace Corps (*peacecorps.gov*) is an international volunteer program run by the U.S. government. The program lasts 27 months and places volunteers in various locations across the world to work in six different sectors ranging from agriculture to education to community economic development. There's no age limit. You are paid a stipend and provided excellent health insurance. Many volunteers are fluent in the local language by the end. Other benefits include student loan deferment and cancelation options.

Why isn't photographer or travel writer listed?

While a good chunk of my income comes from both photography and travel writing, I don't see these as a short-term way to produce income since it's a time-consuming process. I spent years making contacts at the publications I work for regularly. It requires relentless self-promotion and a lot of work. First, you must research publications and find the ones that are the right fit for you. Then, contact them to see how they use photographers and writers. Then, you submit pitches accordingly. Very few publications nowadays will fly you across the world and cover your expenses. Those days are gone. After a pitch is submitted, it can take months for publication and payment. If this interests you, start reaching out to publications months before your trip. Be sure to ask their rates. It's not worth anyone's time to write a 600-word story for $50!

Now, I've given you a huge number of options, so I fully expect you all to go out and start exploring the world! You no longer have any *excuses*!

Where to Teach English

The options are endless for teaching English abroad. I've compiled a list of the most common locations and programs for reference, including links.

Japan

The Jet Program (*jetprogramusa.org*) is the most distinguished English teaching program in the country. Airfare is covered, and the salary is one of the highest in Japan. Housing and transport are subsidized. (A friend who did the program made $33,660 USD/year *tax-free* and only paid $130 USD in rent per month.) The application process is tedious and requires an interview at a Japanese consulate. A Bachelor's degree is required. I applied once, got an interview, but didn't get the job. TIP: If you get an interview, be prepared to answer the following question: What would you say to a student who asked why the U.S. dropped the bomb on Hiroshima? Yes, I was actually asked that question!

Other large teaching programs in Japan include:

- AEON (*aeonet.com*)
- Amity (*amityteachers.com*),
- Altia (*recruiting.altmoot.com*),
- Nova (*nova-holdings.jp/teachinjapan*)
- ECC (*recruiting.ecc.co.jp*).

These are all recommendations from friends who have taught in Japan. For more info on Japan teaching programs and work visas, check out Japan-based expat Tokyo Becky's detailed guide at TokyoBecky.com.

Korea

Most English teaching programs in Korea will cover airfare and accommodation. The application process can take a few months. An FBI background check is required a few months before leaving. (It's not as scary as it sounds.) The best resource for jobs in Korea and other parts of the world is Dave's ESL Café *(eslcafe.com)*. Average salary is roughly $23,000 USD/year. Airfare, housing and visas are covered. Most start dates are in February or August. Many people I know have saved $10,000-$15,000/year teaching in Korea. For more information, check out GoOverseas.com for their guide to teaching in Korea.

Thailand

I taught English briefly through AYC Thailand *(aycthailand.com)* as a substitute kindergarten teacher for a few weeks. Overall, it was a great experience. I've considered doing it again multiple times. I was paid 1,200 Baht/day ($34/USD) but would have made more if I had signed a contract with bonuses. Transport was covered from Bangkok to the teaching location. (I was eight hours away by train in a cool little town called Sisaket.) Since I was only substituting, my accommodation was covered, so I lived on a few dollars a day. (I got free lunch at school.) Salaries are higher, and there are bonuses if you sign a semester contract. Public school semesters run roughly from May to October and November to April. Ajarn.com is a good resource for Thailand job postings. Many of my expat friends living and teaching in Thailand used this site.

Other Locations & Programs

- **Greenheart Travel** *(greenhearttravel.org)* offers programs in Thailand, Europe, Colombia and other parts of the world. (I almost did their Colombia program! The staff is so nice!)

- **VIPKID** *(vipkid.com)* allows you to teach English to kids in China online from your home. Pay rates range from $14-22 USD/hour)

- **Dave's ESL Café** *(eslcafe.com)* also has a great job board for international opportunities across the world.

The Art of Slow Travel

My manager shook his head. He was in his early 30s and had just returned from a two-week vacation. We were chatting about my long-term travels.

"I couldn't travel that long," he said. "I couldn't deal with overindulging in food and all the excess!"

I laughed. That's not how I travel, but it's a constant misconception. Long-term travel isn't a constant indulgence in food, beer, entertainment or anything else. It's about priorities and self-control.

In my opinion, there are three main ways to travel:

Option 1: Work hard all year and splurge all your savings on an elaborate two-week vacation rushing around to see everything.

Option 2: Wait until you are retired and can afford to travel first-class. Spend your retirement years doing all the things you wanted to do when you were younger but didn't have the time or money to do. Cross your fingers, and hope your health holds up.

Option 3: Quit your job or take advantage of any gap of time (weeks, months, or years) to travel long-term across the world slowly on a budget and truly immerse yourself in the culture.

I tried Option 1 for a while, but it isn't my style. Two weeks a year is not enough travel time; I felt too rushed. Option two is risky. What if you don't live that long or your knees give out? Sure, there are people like the Traveling Granny—a 70-year-old from Vancouver who spends four to five months a year traveling solo through either India or Latin America—but people like her are often the exception.

I always call my 78-year-old aunt Sandra for travel advice when I'm contemplating a big adventure. She's a fellow globetrotter and inspired my adventurous spirit. Her response is always the same: "Go now. I would if I could. I have the money to travel first class but don't have the health."

While it's not for everyone, Option 3 has always been the best fit for me. Since I travel for months on end, I can't afford to treat myself to five-star restaurants daily or to live in fancy hotels. Instead, I opt for slow budget travel, which is cheaper in the long run. I stay in hostels, Airbnb rentals, or other types of budget accommodation. I cook, take advantage of restaurant specials, and treat myself on occasion to fancy meals. (Honestly, too much lately.) I take public transport, buses, and trains to take the time to truly see every inch of a country and fully immerse myself in the culture. This allows me to stretch out my savings and truly get to the soul of a place.

It gives me the time to make friends and become part of a place for a short while.

Let's do the math. Traveling for seven months in South America is significantly cheaper than making 14 two-week trips from the U.S. to see the same places. It allows me to relax and get out of my fast-paced American mindset.

I recently went on a luxury boat trip through the Galapagos using a friend's employee discount, which was almost 75 percent off! I was the youngest person on the ship that wasn't a child. Most of the passengers were retired and ranged from age 60-80. During the last night of the trip, people were sharing their highlights. One man said he first heard about the Galapagos in middle school and spent the last 50 years trying to visit! There were 70-somethings chasing sharks with their GoPro cameras while we were snorkeling. It was unbelievable! But they are the lucky ones because they lived long enough to do this trip. This put everything into perspective for me. We aren't all guaranteed to make it age 70 and to be healthy enough to do this trip. It made me extremely grateful to be doing it in my 30s.

I encourage you to find the style of travel that's best for you and don't keep pushing it off. Identify blocks of time that you can allot to a long-term trip, whether it's a cross-country road trip with your kids or spending the summer after college graduation island-hopping in Asia.

Life is short. Go *now*.

Conclusion

Last summer, my best friend Becky casually asked me to climb Mount Kilimanjaro with her in the fall. I laughed at first and made up excuses—it was expensive, and the timing was horrible.

Then, all of a sudden the idea of NOT going seemed the most ridiculous. Physically, I was in the best shape of my life and had just completed my first half-marathon. I had tried for years to get my summer travel job to let me run their Kilimanjaro program without any success. Would I ever get the chance to climb Kilimanjaro with my best friend again? Is the timing ever a 100 percent perfect for anything in life?

After running the numbers, sorting out my teaching schedule and checking flights, I said yes. It wasn't easy, but I made it happen. I aligned my spending habits with my priorities and implemented the savings tactics I had used for years to slash all the costs that weren't fixed. Nothing was going to stand in my way.

I challenge you to do the same with your goals. Let your priorities define your spending habits and slash relentlessly in other areas using the tactics in this book.

Remember these tips apply to more than just travel. Even if I get bored with globetrotting (highly unlikely), then I will use the exact same tactics to pursue another goal like starting that llama petting zoo business I've been joking about for years.

There will always be unavoidable emergencies and occasional splurges. The trick is to not let those moments derail your mindset or spending habits. Focus on the larger goal and take note of the lessons learned.

I've shared all my secrets and a ton of resources with you so you no longer have any excuses so get your finances in order! Start saving!

About the Author

Anna Mazurek is a freelance photographer, writer, and vagabond based in Austin, Texas. She has a Master's degree in photojournalism from the University of Missouri and Bachelor's degree in journalism from the University of South Carolina.

She teaches part-time at the School of Journalism and Mass Communications at Texas State University. She managed summer student photo programs in Asia for five years and currently runs photo trips for National Geographic Student Expeditions.

Anna fell in love with photography and traveling while studying abroad in college. Since then, she's been to 51 countries and lived on four continents. Sitting still is boring.

Her clients include the *Wall Street Journal*, Facebook, Google, *AFAR, Rolling Stone, Travel + Leisure, The Denver Post, The Birmingham News, Austin Monthly, Birmingham* magazine and American Airlines' *American Way* magazine.

To learn more about Anna, please visit the following:

Travel Blog: www.TravelLikeAnna.com
Photography Website: www.AnnaMazurekPhoto.com
Instagram: www.instagram.com/AnnaMazurekPhoto
Twitter: www.twitter.com/TravelLikeAnna

Acknowledgements

Thank you to my family and amazing friends for supporting my travels and unconventional life choices. Thanks to all the people I've met on my travels who made me laugh, gave me advice, or cooked dinner with me. All of these small moments shaped my experiences.

I would like to give a special thanks to Miles Walls for his amazing help editing the text and proofing the book design.

Thank you to all my blog readers and email subscribers. Your support is truly inspirational!

Disclaimer

The information contained in this book is for informational purposes only.

I am not an accountant. Any financial advice I give is my opinion and is informed by my own experiences. By reading this guide, you agree that I am not responsible for financial decisions relating to the content of this book.

I am not employed with any of the brands or companies mentioned in this book. I am not responsible for any transactions with these companies.

No part of this publication shall be reproduced, transmitted, or sold, in whole or in part, in any way, without prior written consent of the author.

Copyright © Anna Mazurek 2018. All Rights Reserved.

Made in the USA
Middletown, DE
23 March 2019